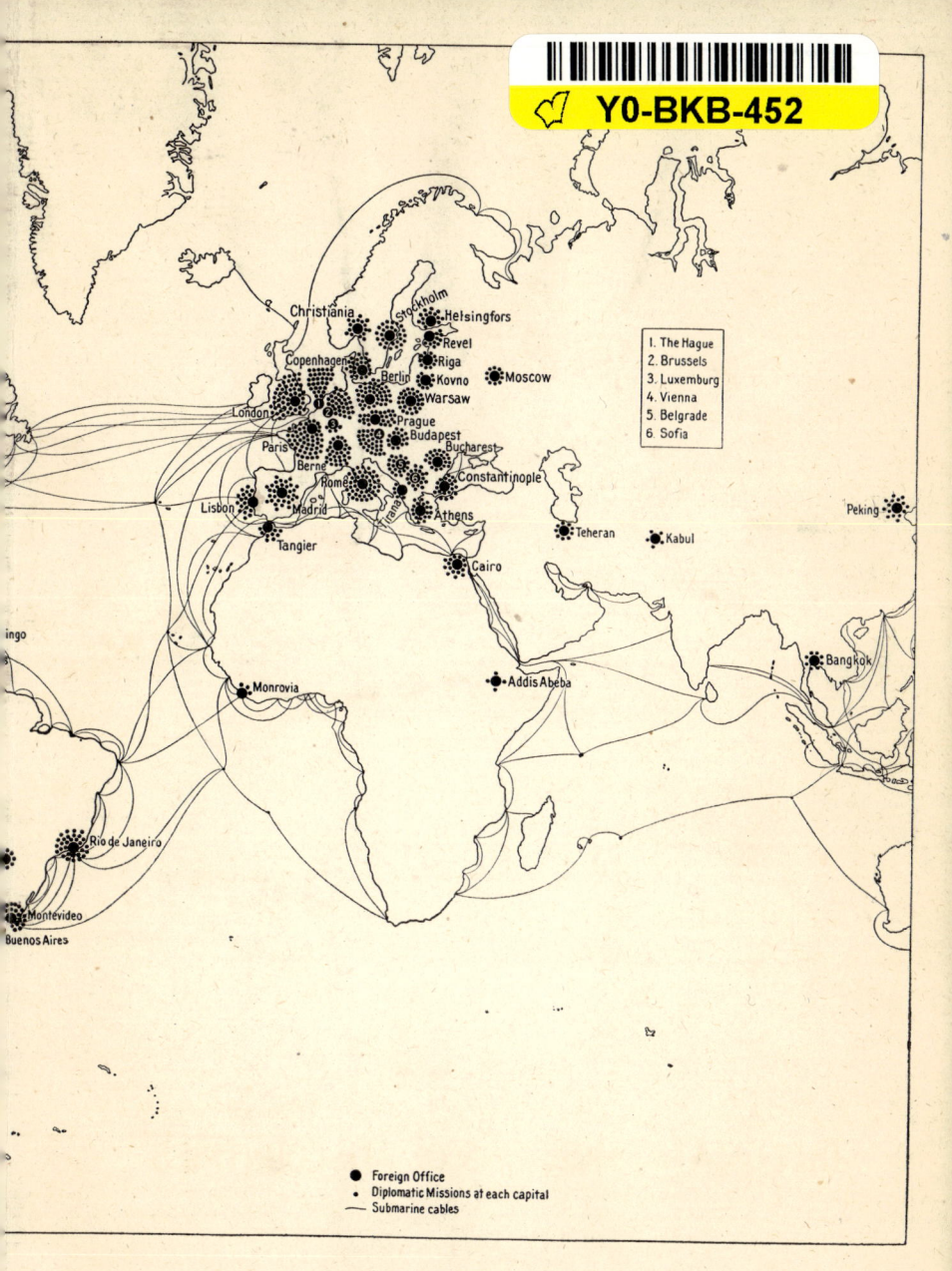

other countries accredited there, as listed in the 1923 edition
of the *Almanach de Gotha*. The light lines on the map indicate the main cable routes of the world.

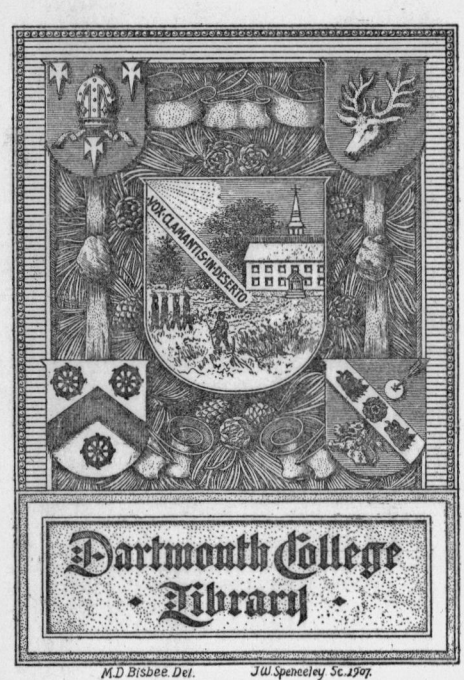

THE INSTITUTE OF POLITICS PUBLICATIONS
WILLIAMS COLLEGE, WILLIAMSTOWN, MASS.

THE CONDUCT OF FOREIGN RELATIONS
UNDER MODERN DEMOCRATIC CONDITIONS

OTHER INSTITUTE OF POLITICS PUBLICATIONS ISSUED BY YALE UNIVERSITY PRESS

ROUND-TABLE CONFERENCES OF THE INSTITUTE OF POLITICS AT ITS FIRST SESSION 1921

THE RECENT AIMS AND POLITICAL DEVELOPMENT OF JAPAN. BY RIKITARO FUJISAWA, Ph.D.

THE PREVENTION OF WAR. BY PHILIP KERR AND LIONEL CURTIS

GERMANY AND EUROPE. BY COUNT HARRY KESSLER

THE
CONDUCT OF FOREIGN RELATIONS UNDER MODERN DEMOCRATIC CONDITIONS

BY
DeWITT C. POOLE
CONSUL GENERAL OF THE UNITED STATES

NEW HAVEN
PUBLISHED FOR THE INSTITUTE OF POLITICS
BY THE YALE UNIVERSITY PRESS
LONDON · HUMPHREY MILFORD · OXFORD UNIVERSITY PRESS
MCMXXIV

Copyright 1924 by Yale University Press.
Printed in the United States of America.

PREFACE

THESE are a series of papers contributed to a Round Table discussion at the Institute of Politics on the subject of *The Conduct of Foreign Relations under Modern Democratic Conditions*. They are based upon some practical experience and such study as could be crowded in with regular official duties. The effort has been to present in logical outline a subject of timely public interest upon which no important treatise has as yet been written. The treatment is of necessity hardly more than suggestive. It is hoped, however, that the sketch of democratic diplomacy in action and of the problem of the democratic control of foreign relations is accurate so far as it goes and will afford the public a readier insight into these important matters than has heretofore been available. The author's best hopes would be fulfilled if this publication would elicit from a more competent quarter the complete and scholarly treatment of the subject which is needed at the earliest possible moment.

It is almost unnecessary to add that statements and opinions are altogether personal and have no necessary connection whatever with the views of the Department of State or of any of its officers. Sources of information have been only those which are open to any diligent student.

I wish to record my appreciation of the personal assistance and encouragement which I have had from my colleagues in the Department of State, from the officers of the Institute of Politics, and from the members of the Round Table, which I had the honor of leading.

D. C. P.

Williamstown, Massachusetts,
  August 25, 1923.

CONTENTS

PART I
Organization and Method in the Conduct of Foreign Relations

CHAPTER	PAGE
I. ESSENTIAL CONDITIONS	3
II. INSTRUMENTALITIES AND PROCESSES	20
III. NATIONAL ORGANIZATION — EUROPEAN DEMOCRACIES	41
IV. NATIONAL ORGANIZATION — THE UNITED STATES	61
V. INTERNATIONAL ORGANIZATION	83

PART II
Democratic Control of Foreign Relations

VI. SECRET AND OPEN DIPLOMACY	93
VII. THE DISSEMINATION OF INFORMATION	110
VIII. PUBLIC OPINION ON FOREIGN AFFAIRS	129
IX. CRYSTALLIZATION AND ENFORCEMENT OF OPINION THROUGH THE LEGISLATURE	143
X. CRYSTALLIZATION AND ENFORCEMENT OF OPINION THROUGH OTHER CHANNELS	170
XI. EFFECTIVENESS AND EFFICIENCY	190
INDEX	199

NOTE.—Maps showing
 (a) the diplomatic and consular offices maintained abroad by the United States, and
 (b) the system of official intercourse among the sovereign states of the world
will be found inside the front and back covers.

PART I
ORGANIZATION AND METHOD IN THE CONDUCT OF FOREIGN RELATIONS

CHAPTER I

ESSENTIAL CONDITIONS

THE foreign affairs of modern democratic states, if they are to be peaceful and succeed, must be conducted with regard to certain essential conditions. These are imposed by the contemporary organization of international society, by the organization of the states themselves, and by human nature.

The essential characteristic of contemporary international society is the absence of a common superior acknowledged by the fifty-odd component states. The pretensions of the head of the Holy Roman Empire to be a super-sovereign and the earlier political authority of the Papacy have ceased. The concept of the sovereignty or supreme authority of the individual states has supervened instead and underlies the theory and practice of international intercourse. It is not necessary for us to attempt to define this concept fully.[1] For our purpose it may be accepted as meaning that each of the states making up international society—the conduct of whose mutual relations we are about to study—is to itself the supreme authority, that there is no acknowledged superior over them all, that each reserves to itself the ultimate judgment of its rights and obligations toward its fellows.

From this order of things it follows, first, that each state, as a phase of its sovereign character, enjoys independence in its internal affairs. A state can adopt

[1] See Oppenheim: *International law,* 3d ed., 1: 125-133, and other standard works on international law.

any constitution it likes, arrange its administration in any way it thinks fit, enact such laws as it pleases, adopt any commercial policy. It is only in certain special cases or when these acts impinge directly upon the rights of other states or their citizens that they may be called into question internationally. This has come out clearly in the recent relations of the United States and Russia. The confiscatory measures adopted by the Russian Soviet régime against citizens of Russia itself were not the concern of the United States. The United States has taken, and could properly take, these measures into account only so far as they impaired the existing and justly acquired rights of American citizens.

Likewise a sovereign state enjoys external independence. It can manage its international affairs according to discretion. It can enter into alliances and conclude other treaties, send and receive diplomatic envoys, acquire and cede territory, make war and peace. Other states may not interfere unless their interests are directly affected. If, as a result of this independent action, difficulties arise between two states, third states, though they deem their interests to be indirectly involved, may not intervene unless asked or expressly permitted to do so. This has been amply illustrated by current events in Europe. Mr. Root recently explained the matter in concrete terms. "A lot of people," he said, "wanted us to stop France from going into the Ruhr. We have no more right to do that than France would have to come over here and make us naturalize the Japanese. Many people who realized that wanted us to mediate between Germany and France. We had no right to do that unless they were willing and an inquiry was made, apparently, to ascertain whether they were and it seemed that they were not. That ended it. That stopped us unless we were willing to violate rights of France and Germany which we would not permit them to violate in our case."[2]

A second consequence of the sovereignty of states of fundamental importance in diplomacy is the rule of unanimity. It is plain that while peace prevails the common affairs of sovereign states can move only by general agreement. At international conferences, or in other multi-party negotiations, the views of a majority have only a persuasive force. They do not prevail of their own right as they would in a domestic legislative assembly. The efforts of the Hague Conference of 1907 to establish a general system of arbitration were wrecked by the opposition of Germany and Austria. At the Washington Conference a majority of the participating Powers seemed ready to discuss the limitation of land as well as naval armament, but one Power felt—no doubt quite rightly—that its vital interests would not permit the further reduction of its land forces at that time, and the point was perforce passed without further discussion. It is necessary to bear this always in mind. While states remain sovereign, general agreement must be an essential condition to

[2] Address at Washington, Jan. 17, 1923, before Committee of One Hundred of the American Civic Federation, as reported in New York *Times* for Jan. 18, 1923.

Concerning independence as an aspect of sovereignty, see Oppenheim, *op. cit.*, 1: 206 ff., espc. 207; and Hyde: *International law*, 1: 84 ff. On the subject of intervention, see Oppenheim, 1: 221 ff.; Hyde, 1: 116 ff.; and Stowell, E. C.: *Intervention in international law* (Washington, 1921).

the progress of their common affairs. The *liberum veto* rules diplomacy and may at any time baffle effective achievement. The difficulty is not always understood by citizens at home. If a national desire has been defeated or delayed, feeling is engendered among those who might be first to resist an encroachment upon the sovereign rights of their own country.

The rule of unanimity is supplemented by a third important consequence of the sovereignty of states, namely, the principle of equality. The principle of equality has been much debated. It used to be argued that sovereign states were equal in a general sense, that equality emanated naturally from their common sovereign and independent character, but this doctrine has not held up in the face of manifest inequalities of material endowment and political capacity. The primacy of certain Powers has long been recognized. At the time of the Congress of Vienna in 1815, eight states—Austria, France, Great Britain, Portugal, Prussia, Russia, Spain, and Sweden—were recognized as the Great Powers. Their number was reduced to five when Portugal, Spain, and Sweden lost that character. Italy was added after its unification. The United States rose as a Great Power (in the opinion of Oppenheim) out of the Civil War, and Japan out of the war with China. There were then eight Great Powers, of which the six in Europe were known as the European Concert. Since 1918 the defeat of the Central Powers and the breakdown of Russia have placed leadership in the hands of the five which are described in the treaties of peace as the Principal Allied and Associated Powers, namely, the United States, France, Great Britain, Italy, and Japan.

The theory of the equality of states nevertheless survives in law and to some extent in diplomacy. In the latter respect it has been spoken of as "little more than a matter of courtesy and good form," but it goes further than that. It follows from the legal principle of the equality of states that, whenever a question arises which has to be settled by the consent of the members of the family of nations, every state has a right to a vote, but to one vote only. A second consequence is that legally the vote of the weakest and smallest state has quite as much weight as the vote of the largest and most powerful. Therefore any alteration of an existing rule or creation of a new rule of international law by a law-making treaty has legal validity for the signatory powers and those only who later accede expressly or submit to it tacitly through custom.

Such is the law as stated by Oppenheim. The same holds true in a political sense, only less positively. At an international conference, or in ordinary diplomatic negotiation, it is plain that the opinions and desires of Great Powers may be more influential than those of their lesser brethren. But, as international affairs proceed only by the consent of all concerned, the vote or assent of one of the smaller states may be hardly less necessary than that of a Great Power in order to arrive at an effective result. Action generally approved or desired may be delayed or prevented by the negative attitude of a minor state having a relatively unimportant interest in the matter. Unless covertly supported by one or more Great Powers, the minor state may not deem it politically expedient to persist in opposition, but the possibility of its doing so is one of the realities of diplomacy and tends to equalize the position of all in the family of nations.[3]

How then, granted divergencies of purpose and interest, is agreement obtainable among sovereign states without the direct use of force? The primary actuating motive in state policy is self-interest. Self-interest may be approached in various ways. On the one hand we have the threat of force and related maneuvers, such as economic pressure, which derive their ultimate effectiveness from force; on the other hand, there are the common interests and conciliation and adjustment.

Many believe that the threat of force is the only real basis of successful negotiation. To be effective beyond a certain limited range, it has been said that diplomacy "rests, and can only rest, on the implication of force." Another has said: "The strength of diplomatic representations is always in direct ratio to the force behind." Lorimer, in *The Institutes of the Law of Nations,* writes: "Force is the bullion on which international credit depends, and fear is its circulating medium."[4] These blunt statements bring

[3] On the equality of states, see Oppenheim, *op. cit.*, 1: 196 ff.; Hyde, *op. cit.*, 1: 20 ff.; and Dickinson, E. D.: *The equality of states in international law* (Cambridge, 1920). The doctrine of equality in law has not gone unchallenged. As long ago as 1885 T. J. Lawrence expressed the opinion that in view of the hegemony of the Great Powers it was "impossible to hold any longer the old doctrine of the absolute equality of all independent states before the law." *The primacy of the great powers,* in *Essays on some disputed questions in modern international law,* p. 232.

[4] The preceding quotations are respectively from Brooks, Sydney: *American foreign policy,* in *English Rev.,* 9: 682 (Nov., 1911), and Blennerhasset, Sir Rowland: *Foreign policy,* in *Fort. Rev.,* 91 (N. S. 85): 625 (April, 1909).

an unpleasant shock, and I doubt that they are unqualifiedly true. It would be unintelligent, however, to belittle the direct relationship between the show of military force and national prestige. A member of the delegation which was sent to the United States in 1921 by the Far Eastern Republic passed through Moscow a year later on the return trip to his country. Speaking to the Soviet press of what the delegation had accomplished in the United States, he said: "It should be noted that, as in the case of every success of the Red Army, the victories of the Workmen-Peasants' army of the Far Eastern Republic also had an immediate effect on the attitude of different groups in the United States toward the delegation, and, in increasing the delegation's significance, thereby facilitated its work."[5] For our own part we have but to recall the cruise of the American fleet around the world in 1908. This and the digging of the Panama Canal were the two American achievements, in Mr. Roosevelt's opinion, which really impressed foreign peoples during the first dozen years of the century.[6]

While states remain sovereign and peoples frequently selfish and sometimes wrong-headed, force is plainly the ultimate arbiter, and the threat of its use in one way or another the most direct and cogent appeal to self-interest. A widening intelligence, more intimate international relationships, and the vastly increasing cost of force more and more, however, dispose governments to purely pacific methods. With each generation the community of interests among states is more keenly felt. "Though the individual

[5] Moscow *Izvestia*, Sept. 8, 1922.
[6] Theodore Roosevelt: *An autobiography*, p. 595.

States are sovereign and independent of each other,'' writes Oppenheim,[7] "though there is no international Government above the national ones, though there is no central political authority to which the different states are subjected, yet there is something mightier than all the powerful separating factors: namely, the common interests.'' The readiness of states to serve the common interests, as an enlightened means to ultimate self-interest, gives life to international law and comity, while a growing sense of the community of civilization forms the basis of that world public opinion which more and more makes itself felt in the councils of statesmen and in the thought of peoples.

In the same way conciliation and adjustment are fostered. Their most elementary and material form is diplomatic bargaining. Germany is given Heligoland in order that Britain may have more of Africa. It is easy to be cynical about this, but when it is done openly and with due respect for the rights of others, it is merely legitimate barter; the alternative may be force. But there is a higher form of conciliation which becomes increasingly operative in international affairs. If we look back over a considerable period we cannot fail to note a growing readiness among states to sacrifice expediency to principle on the ground of ultimate advantage; to forego immediate gains for later and more substantial benefits; to recognize fairness as a policy which pays in the long run. Mr. Hughes said recently: "It must be remembered that only a small portion of the controversial matters of great consequence, which are

[7] *Op. cit.*, 1: 10.

now engaging the attention of Foreign Offices, admit the application of juridical standards. They are matters demanding not legal decisions but adjustments by mutual consent. In this world of intimate relations, you are likely to have either hostility or cooperation. There is no artificial method by which adjustments can be reached in the absence of a sincere desire for accord, and the cultivation of the spirit of mutual friendliness is thus the primary consideration. . . . The nation that can most easily settle its differences and promote its interests, the nation that can look most hopefully for a recognition of its claims, is the nation that by its reasonable and friendly disposition, its poise and sense of justice, inspires confidence and wins esteem."[8]

This enlightened view is gaining among the nations, but we cannot be too sanguine. After the Paris Peace Conference Mr. Lansing wrote: "When we come to formulate our foreign policies upon the belief that justice in the abstract is a dominant force in the regulation of world affairs, we are building on a foundation which, however desirable, is by no means certain. We must recognize the fact, unpalatable though it may be, that nations to-day are influenced more by selfishness than by an altruistic sentiment of justice. The time may come when the nations will change their present attitude through a realization that uniform justice in foreign as well as domestic affairs is the highest type of expediency; but that time has not yet come, and, if we are wise, we will not deceive ourselves by assuming that the

[8] *Some observations on the conduct of our foreign relations,* in *Am. Jour. Int. Law,* 16: 371 (July, 1922).

policies of other Governments are founded on unselfishness or on a constant purpose to be just even though the consequences be contrary to their immediate interests.'"[9]

A second set of conditions affecting the intercourse of modern democratic states springs from their own internal organization. A state, as a member of international society, is a unit and continuous in its existence, but it is represented concretely by a government which is but a temporary organ for the exercise of its sovereignty.[10] While governments of all types are relatively transitory and the play of domestic politics may break through the most autocratic façade, democratic government, with its checks and balances and brief bestowals of authority, is by its very nature especially removed from the theoretical nature of the state as an international person. The executive branch of government represents usually one party or group of parties and in unity of thought and action approaches closest to the international ideal, but it is withal only an aggregate of individuals, each primarily intent upon the work of his particular department; and, while in international affairs the foreign minister acts for the whole government, his colleagues may not always be amenable to the suggestions which he makes in the interest of international advantage. Mr. Page has described the difficulties which Sir Edward Grey experienced during the early part of the World War to maintain friendly relations with the United States while his military and naval colleagues were loath

[9] Cited in Hyde, *op. cit.*, 1: 21.
[10] *Cf.* Oppenheim, *op. cit.*, 1: 132; and Moore: *Digest of international law,* 1: 40.

to forego any measures which might make the blockade of Germany more effective.[11]

Breaches of unity between the executive and legislative branches of governments are more frequently observable. They are by no means confined to the United States. One need but recall the case of the Declaration of London, when the British House of Lords effectively negatived an international act to which the executive branch was committed.[12] In parliamentary governments the possibility of a ministerial upset is always present. The ministry which speaks for a country today may not be in power tomorrow, and policies which it has supported may be abandoned or less earnestly pursued. Mr. Lloyd George reached an understanding on the European situation with M. Briand at Cannes in January, 1922, as a result of which the latter almost immediately retired from office in favor of his political opponent, M. Poincaré, and the chances of success for the ensuing conference at Genoa, for which Mr. Lloyd George had such hopeful expectations, were thereby much reduced.[13]

These are essential conditions in the conduct of foreign affairs among democratic states. A foreign secretary must take account of domestic politics not only in his own country but also in those with which he is dealing. The foreign secretary of another country who is hampered by unwilling cabinet colleagues must be allowed as far as possible to work out his difficulties in his own way. If a ministry of the day is favorable to some matter in hand, negotia-

---

[11] Hendrick: *Life and letters of Walter H. Page,* 1: 364 ff.
[12] See *infra,* pp. 67 ff.
[13] *Current History,* 15: 867 and 878 (Feb., 1922).

tions must be conducted, if possible, so as to strengthen, or at least not to damage, its internal political position. At the same time the aspect of unity must be preserved at home. Mr. Lansing recounts that, after President Wilson had apparently failed during his visit to the United States early in 1919 to rally to the support of the Covenant of the League such an overwhelming popular sentiment as the opposition in the Senate could not resist, the peoples of Europe and their statesmen lost a measure of their enthusiasm and faith in the project.[14]

The conduct of foreign relations, like domestic politics, is an intensely human business. More fundamental than the conditions which we have already noted are those, finally, which are imposed by human nature itself. Back of governments is humanity; and humanity is divided into many individual and self-assertive groups, to whom self-preservation is the first law and expansion the natural impulse. Aggressive nationalism is the primordial force with which modern diplomacy has to cope. The nations have been formed by various influences, among which are race, language, and long association. The essence of their nationalism is sentiment. Each has developed in the course of history a particular psychology. Each has acquired its own modes of thought and feeling, its conceptions of what is right and decent, its conception of what constitutes liberty and what constitutes right between man and man. These conceptions differ profoundly. What seems self-evident to one group is unintelligible or repugnant to another. The Anglo-Saxon, the Latin, the

[14] Lansing: *The peace negotiations*, p. 143.

Slav, the Oriental, and the lesser divisions among them move by different processes. Not only do they speak different languages. They do not have the same standards of honor or humor, nor reach like conclusions from the same premises. Unreasoning patriotism, the contempt and distrust of foreigners, and indifference to the rights of others are universal.[15]

So intense an individualism renders mutual understanding among peoples difficult and fosters sensitiveness and pride. States wear their honor on their sleeve and reserve full liberty of action in any affair which is deemed to touch it.[16] Tact and courtesy become of the first importance in negotiation, and restraint in the public criticism of foreign nations the duty of every peace-loving citizen.[17]

---

[15] See address of Mr. Root cited above; Brown, P. M.: *International society*, chap. I and p. 117; and Muir, Ramsay: *Nationalism and internationalism* (London, 1917), pp. 37 ff.

[16] Arbitration conventions customarily except, by express provision, questions affecting "the vital interests, the independence, or the honor" of the contracting states. *Cf.* Convention of June 4, 1908, between the United States and Great Britain, Malloy: *Treaties*, 1: 814.

[17] Both Mr. Hughes and Mr. Root have recently spoken with much emphasis of this duty. See Hughes: *Some observations on the conduct of our foreign relations*, in *Am. Jour. Int. Law*, 16: 370-372 (July, 1922); and Root: *A requisite for the success of popular diplomacy*, in *Foreign Affairs* (N. Y.), 1: 9 (Sept., 1922). Mr. Root writes: "Nations are even more sensitive to insult than individuals. One of the most useful and imperative lessons learned by all civilized governments in the practice of international intercourse has been the necessity of politeness and restraint in expression. Without these, the peaceful settlement of controversy is impossible. This lesson should be learned by every free democracy which seeks to control foreign relations."

It must always be borne in mind that the statesmen of democracies are not acting for themselves or for a single master, but for their fellow-citizens. They are the agents and the advocates of their people, and their people expect them to obtain results. One of the chief obstacles to the peaceful adjustment of international controversies, in Mr. Root's opinion, is the fact that the negotiator or arbitrator who yields any part of the extreme claims of his country and concedes the reasonableness of any argument of the other side is quite likely to be violently condemned by great numbers of his own countrymen who have not taken the pains to make themselves familiar with the merits of the controversy or have considered only the arguments on their side. "Sixty-four years have passed," Mr. Root wrote in 1905, "since the northeastern boundary between the United States and Canada was settled by the Webster-Ashburton treaty of 1842; yet to this day there are many people on our side of the line who condemn Mr. Webster for sacrificing our rights, and many people on the Canadian side of the line who blame Lord Ashburton for sacrificing their rights, in that treaty. Both sets of objectors cannot be right; it seems a fair inference that neither of them is right; yet both Mr. Webster and Lord Ashburton had to endure reproach and obloquy as the price of agreeing upon a settlement which has been worth to the peace and prosperity of each country a thousand times as much as the value of all the territory that was in dispute."[18]

These are the essential conditions, very briefly

[18] *The need for a popular understanding of international law,* in *Am. Jour. Int. Law,* 1:1.

ESSENTIAL CONDITIONS

indicated, which confront a citizen, when, having been named secretary of state or minister of foreign affairs, he sets out to conduct the foreign relations of his country. What guides has he in the performance of his duties?

He has in general two kinds of matters to deal with—those that fall in the realm of high policy, and those that make up the day-to-day administration of the country's foreign business. There are few routine matters in a foreign office. What seems a trifling matter at the start may kindle suddenly into a burning issue.

The main lines of the foreign policies of nations seem frequently to be determined by the circumstances of their existence and reassert themselves in a surprising way under the greatest diversity of governments and personalities. The French Revolution did not alter permanently the fundamentals of French foreign policy.[19] One of the most interesting phenomena of the Russian Revolution is the reversion of the Soviets to the main lines of the foreign policy of the Tsars. An American secretary of state is familiar, when he assumes office, with the guiding principles of American policy, and the same may be predicated generally. Thus certain guideposts exist for basic policy, though from time to time new alternatives present themselves, as when England forewent isolation for the Entente Cordiale and the United States held aloof from the League of Nations.

For the less basic matters that crowd a foreign office day by day the responsible officials have also

[19] Cf. Sorel: *L'Europe et la revolution française*, 2: 106; 3: 392; 4: 174 and 8: 507.

the test of these guiding principles. They have recourse to international law, which contains the peaceful solvent of many questions, and to the rules of comity. Most foreign ministries have a vast accumulation of precedents. Those of the American State Department were gathered up by John Bassett Moore in 1906 in his monumental *Digest of International Law*.

The successful application of principles and precedents to particular international problems as they arise plainly calls for an extraordinary combination of legal acumen, political judgment, and human understanding. A foreign minister, unlike his colleagues in the cabinet, is dealing not with one government and one people but with fifty governments and fifty peoples of the greatest imaginable physical and psychological variety. He deals, like the physician, with difficulties arising from causes beyond his control. The material facts of problems form but the basis of his calculations. He must find an answer in the weighing of imponderables.

And there is the pressure of time. Often it is of the essence of a proposed solution that it be applied at once. A situation exists at a given moment which seems to admit of or require a particular course of action. In a few days or a few hours it will be different. The moment will have passed. Among the failures of diplomacy are many right solutions applied too late.

John Hay wrote: "It is abominable form for a government to brag of its diplomatic success." To refer to difficulties solved may be but to revive them in a new and aggravated shape. The daily achievements of diplomacy in facilitating the intercourse of states and removing the causes of irritation among peoples must go for the most part unnoticed. The failures stand out. Self-elimination in the service of his country, it has been said, is the duty of the diplomatist no less than of the soldier.

CHAPTER II

INSTRUMENTALITIES AND PROCESSES

THE organization regularly employed by the fifty-odd sovereign states for the conduct of business among themselves rests on the constitutional structure of each but manifests itself on the international plane as a substantially uniform world system. Each state maintains—at home, a department or ministry of foreign affairs headed by a member of the cabinet; abroad, a foreign service of greater or less extent, embracing diplomatic and consular branches. The minister of foreign affairs formulates foreign policy, subject to the control in varying measure of the head of the state, the cabinet, and the legislature. He receives the communications of the foreign diplomatic representatives at his capital and instructs the representatives of his own government abroad as to the communications which they are to make to the governments to which they are accredited. He is usually aided by a vice minister or under secretary, several assistant ministers or secretaries, and a corps of specialists—political, economic, and legal—drawn frequently from the ranks of the foreign service after actual duty in the field and organized within the ministry in geographical and topical divisions.

Abroad a country's representation in the territory of any other particular country consists normally of a diplomatic mission at the capital and consular offices at the principal centres, especially the commercial centres, which may include the capital also.

The diplomatic mission varies in composition with the volume and importance of the business to be done. At its head is an ambassador, minister, or *chargé d'affaires*. In addition there are usually one or more secretaries, who are subordinate diplomatic officials apart from the clerical staff, performing such duties as are assigned to them by the head of the mission. There may also be military, naval, commercial, and other attachés, who occupy themselves with, and may advise the head of the mission in regard to, the concerns of the particular home departments (War, Navy, Commerce, etc.) at whose instance they have been appointed.

The American Foreign Service comprised at a recent date 51 diplomatic missions and 411 consular offices.[1] The services of the other Great Powers are

[1] In an official announcement, April 27, 1921, concerning entrance examinations, the Department of State explained: "The Diplomatic and Consular Services, known sometimes collectively as the Foreign Service, constitute the field force for the conduct of the foreign relations of the United States. The work of the two services is in many respects closely allied. The Diplomatic Service is charged with the conduct of official intercourse between the Government of the United States and the other governments of the world. . . . It is the duty of a (diplomatic) mission, in addition to serving as the official channel of communication between our Government and the government to which it is accredited, to protect the lives and property of American citizens, to observe and report to the Secretary of State upon political and other conditions in the country of its residence, and, in conjunction with the Consular Service, to safeguard and promote the general and commercial interests of the United States and of individual citizens."

"The Consular Service," the announcement continued, "shares with the Diplomatic Service the duty of protecting the lives and property of American citizens abroad; both are actively concerned of similar extent. In all there are about 1,100 diplomatic missions and 6,000 or 7,000 consulates functioning in the world today. The map inside the front cover of this volume shows the disposition of the 1,100 diplomatic missions at the 50-odd capitals of the world. The number at each capital corresponds, of course, to its political importance. The concentration in Western Europe is very striking. The map inside the back cover shows the disposition abroad of the Foreign Service of the United States, both diplomatic missions and consulates. A similar map showing those of all countries with a line from each to its respective Foreign Ministry at home would serve as an official nerve chart in an anatomy of the world's affairs. If there could be added the unofficial contacts, such as those of the press and of international business, the whole extent and complexity of the world's nervous system would be revealed.

Diplomacy as it interests the public consists of the salient problems which emerge from the welter of

with safeguarding and promoting the general and commercial interests of the nation and of individual Americans; and they collaborate in observing and reporting upon conditions in the countries of their residence. In these fields of common endeavor, the work of the two services is coördinated in each country. Consuls deal with matters involving relations with local authorities, while the diplomatic mission deals with those requiring contact with the central authorities. The diplomatic mission is concerned, primarily, but by no means exclusively, with political affairs, while consuls give their more special attention to investigations and reports of an economic nature, and to assisting individual American exporters in the extension of their foreign trade. Consuls also perform important administrative functions, and act in general as the business, as distinguished from the political, agents of the Government."

international activity which this system of intercommunication suggests, though upon the efficient and friendly despatch of lesser matters frequently depends the tone of relations existing between particular governments and peoples and consequently the ready and peaceful disposition of major problems as they arise. It is the handling of the major problems which determines the course of foreign policy.

The direction of foreign policy is perforce committed to a few hands. Those who exercise an important and more or less constant influence upon it in any given country at any given period may include:

At home, the head of the state, the premier, the minister of foreign affairs, and half a dozen principal assistants and advisers, and a few others such as other members of the cabinet and leaders in the legislature—say, fifteen at the most;

Abroad, the heads of the more important and influential diplomatic missions, who would not number more than five for any one country at any one time.

Counting fifty countries we arrive by approximation at a total of 1,000 individuals, who may be said to exercise a direct and continuous influence during any given period of comparative peace on the course of international relations. If the count be limited to the five Great Powers which seem now to exercise a dominant influence in world politics, the number is at most 100.

This restriction of leadership and responsibility has its parallel in other fields of government. It is interesting in relation to foreign affairs principally because the system, or the individuals concerned, become at certain crises an object of public criticism. Complaint is directed against "diplomacy" or "the diplomats." The latter term has certainly no very clear definition in the minds of many who use it, but may be presumed to indicate those, especially in the older countries, who have devoted their lives to diplomacy and are popularly regarded as making up an exclusive caste of aristocratic tendencies removed from the influences of everyday life and democratic progress. It is interesting, therefore, in connection with a study of diplomacy and democracy to determine how many of the individuals actually charged at some recent date with the conduct of the foreign affairs of the dominant World Powers might, so far as one may judge from their records, be considered "diplomats" in this sense. How many of them were instead merely public men indistinguishable in essentials from others who have arrived at positions of responsibility in the normal course of government?

The Foreign Ministers of the United States, France, Great Britain, Italy, and Japan listed in the 1922 edition of the *Almanach de Gotha* were Hughes, Poincaré, Curzon, Torretta, and Uchida. Of these, the last two only may be characterized as diplomats of career. It is a fair assumption that the heads of state, other cabinet members, and legislators having weight in the formulation of foreign policy were almost exclusively public men without a special diplomatic background. On the other hand, the Vice Ministers or Under Secretaries of Foreign Affairs listed for the five principal powers in the 1922 *Almanach de Gotha* were all of the diplomatic category, and of the twenty Ambassadors exchanged by these five powers in 1922 fourteen were diplomats of career. The exceptions were the four Ambassadors of the United States and the representatives of Great Britain and Italy at Washington. The preponderance of career diplomats in the less important posts was doubtless greater.[2]

Assuming that this was a typical situation, it appears, first, that the formulation of important policies at the great capitals is normally in the hands of public men who may be politicians or statesmen, but not diplomats in any special sense. This is important. Critics of "diplomacy" seem sometimes to forget that with modern methods of communication the actual determination of policy, even in relative detail, lies not with the diplomatic representative abroad, but with the minister of foreign affairs at home, who is a member of the government of the day, or with the cabinet or the head of the state. The second deduction is that the execution of policy abroad is for the most part in trained professional hands.

This would seem to be a satisfactory situation. Conditions vary, of course, in different countries. In Mr. Hughes' opinion, recently expressed, the organization of American instrumentalities of foreign intercourse has rather suffered from too much re-

[2] The Vice Ministers or Under Secretaries were: United States, Henry P. Fletcher; Great Britain, Sir J. Eyre Crowe; Italy, Valvassari Peroni; Japan, Hanihara. There was a vacancy in France, but the incumbency of a trained diplomat may be assumed.

The following were the ambassadors of the Great Powers at the respective capitals, according to the 1922 *Almanach de Gotha:* Washington—Jusserand, Geddes, Ricci, Shidehara; Paris—Herrick, Hardinge, Sforza, Ishii; London—Harvey, Saint Aulaire, Martino, Hayashi; Rome—Child, Mallet, Barrère, Otchiai; Tokyo —Warren, Claudel, Eliot, Aliotti.

gard for politicians and too little attention to the necessity for special aptitude and training.[3] Even those who might deprecate the presence of two career diplomats among the Foreign Ministers of the five Great Powers in 1922 must recall that a diplomat of the bureaucratic type is restricted in his potentialities for harm by the very measure of his deficiencies. The careers are open to talent nowadays. Men, like Torretta in Italy, who climb the diplomatic ladder to positions of political influence, do so by reason of qualities which tend strongly to negative the professional limitations which may characterize their less successful colleagues. It is true that there has been in many countries until recent years—in some countries still—something of a diplomatic caste, or at least caste feeling, the vestiges of which, lingering in the lesser ranks of diplomacy, may account for adverse criticism; but an analysis of existing conditions tends to the conclusion that those who are dealing with substantive international policy are not distinguishable essentially from leaders in other fields of government and that their virtues and shortcomings are those of politicians and statesmen generally.

One special fact should, however, be noted. In no branch of public life are the demands on the purse of the individual so heavy as in the field of foreign representation. This is so much the case that only when governments provide large salaries and liberal special allowances can any but the rich undertake diplomatic posts or accept comfortably the position of foreign minister at home. It is the democracies,

[3] *Some observations on the conduct of our foreign relations*, in *Am. Jour. Int. Law* (July, 1922), 16: 366.

among them the United States, which, with a readily understood inconsistency, have been conspicuous in creating through niggardliness this artificial barrier to the natural democratic selection of leaders in the field of foreign affairs.[4]

The chief duties of a foreign diplomatic representative have been summed up by an experienced American diplomatist[5] under the heads of vigilance,

[4] *Cf.* statements by Mr. Hughes in an address before the Chamber of Commerce of the United States on *Some aspects of the work of the Department of State.* He said: "The Diplomatic Service is greatly underpaid. A man of moderate means, whatever his ability, cannot accept the more important posts of Ambassador or Minister. These high offices are reserved to men of wealth, when in the interest of the country they should be within the reach of men of ability, whatever their private fortune. Certainly they should be within the reach of men of talent who have ignored the opportunities to amass wealth by reason of their long employment in the service of their country.

"The salaries are so low in the classified Diplomatic Service that the choice of candidates is largely restricted to young men of wealthy families who are able and willing to a considerable extent to pay their own way. It is a most serious thing to be compelled to say that a young man without means, who desires to marry and bring up a family after the American tradition, cannot be encouraged to enter upon one of the most important careers that the country has to offer. I say bluntly that no American can face the facts without a sense of humiliation, and he is compelled to qualify his boasting of our intelligence and civilization so long as this condition continues." *Am. Jour. Int. Law* (July, 1922), 16: 362.

Mr. Bryan excused the continuance of his Chautauqua lectures while Secretary of State on the ground that his official salary was inadequate to life in Washington and the requirements of his position.

[5] Dr. David Jayne Hill. See his article, *Shall we standardize our Diplomatic Service,* in *Harper's Magazine* (April, 1914), 128: 690, for a good informal exposition of the demands made in

advice, and negotiation—*vigilance* to observe and report to his government everything which it might profit by knowing with respect to conditions, events, opinions, and tendencies in the country of his residence; *advice* with regard to current diplomatic business based on an intimate knowledge of local conditions and affairs. The formal relations of the diplomatic agent are only with the ministry of foreign affairs, or occasionally with the chief of state, but his duties of vigilance and advice necessitate an extensive informal relationship with other branches of the executive, with individual members of the legislature, with the press, and with private citizens.

Negotiation is the normal course of international business, the solvent to which all questions are subjected in the preliminary stages. Only the few which prove refractory to this process become the occasion for good offices or mediation, the subject of an arbitration,[6] or the cause of war, which marks diplomacy's failure. Negotiations may proceed orally or in writing or by both methods. When conversations occur, each party prepares memoranda of them for his own use, and the results of conversations may be reduced to writing and mutually agreed to. In general the processes of diplomacy are essentially the

practice upon a diplomatist. For a more formal and legal statement of the functions of a minister, see Hyde: *International law,* 1: 763-775.

[6] *Cf.* Moore: *Specific agencies for the proper conduct of international relations,* in Walsh: *History and nature of international relations.* Professor Moore gives a brief account in this article of good offices, mediation, and arbitration. He lists these with negotiation as the peaceful methods of conducting international relations.

same as the processes of business among individuals, only more careful and formal, as becomes diplomacy's greater importance, being the business of many individuals.

The forms of international agreement and contract vary, according to the nature and importance of the matter, from simple memoranda to treaties in full form. Satow[7] mentions fifteen different forms of international agreement and contract. There may also be "understandings." Recent times have brought a great increase in treaty-making. An American scholar computed in 1917 that 25,000 treaties were then in existence, of which two-fifths were in force. He estimated that the last century had produced more treaties than all the past. The rapid extension of treaty-making is reflected in our own experience. The framers of the Constitution did not anticipate or desire the conclusion of many treaties; yet up to the end of the last century the United States had averaged more than four treaties a year, and in the present century it has averaged fifteen a year or a treaty ratified every three weeks.[8]

Diplomacy does not hesitate, as special exigencies arise, to supplement its normal processes by recourse to extraordinary instrumentalities and methods. Consuls, who have not normally the full representative character, become, when circumstances require, quasi-diplomatic agents. Those at the capitals of the self-governing Dominions of the British Empire and similar posts are almost con-

[7] *Diplomatic practice,* 1st ed., 2: 173.
[8] Myers, D. P.: *The control of foreign relations,* in *Am. Pol. Sci. Rev.,* 11: 31 (Feb., 1917); and Wright, Quincy: *The control of American foreign relations,* pp. 246 and 247.

stantly in this situation, and in troubled areas such as Mexico and Russia consular officers may play important diplomatic rôles. The occasional diplomatic activities of American naval officers are well known.[9] The commanders of military forces in time of war may exercise quasi-diplomatic functions. Unofficial persons are also employed for diplomatic errands, clandestine or avowed. In America special attention has been drawn to this mode of procedure in recent years by the activities of John Lind and William Bayard Hale in Mexico and of Colonel House in Europe. The American system of "unofficial observers" was quickly developed in order to meet a new and extraordinary situation. In the practice of foreign countries reference may be made to the cases of M. Franklin Bouillon, French emissary to Angora, and M. Herriot, Mayor of Lyons, who visited Moscow in the summer of 1922. Both of these gentlemen are officials, but M. Herriot's Moscow trip was never admitted to have had a diplomatic purpose, and it is said that M. Franklin Bouillon did not take on the public character of an official representative until he had succeeded in establishing friendly relations with Kemal.

An interesting illustration of diplomacy's readiness to work with the instruments at hand is found in the frequency with which the press now serves in effect as an unofficial diplomatic agency, becoming a vehicle for what are known in diplomatic parlance as *ballons d'essai*. These "trial balloons" are especially to be observed at international conferences.

[9] See Paullin: *Diplomatic negotiations of American naval officers* (Baltimore, 1912) and Chester: *Diplomacy of the quarter-deck*, in *Am. Jour. Int. Law*, 8: 443.

A delegation, desiring to test the general acceptability of some idea, inspires one or more representatives of the press to put it out in the guise of a rumor or prophecy of impending action and is then enabled to watch the effect on the conference generally or on particular delegations. At one stage of the Washington Armament Conference an important delegation (not the Japanese) persistently conveyed to the press the idea that the conference would or should adjourn without entering upon the delicate question created by the continued presence of Japanese troops in Eastern Siberia. The issue was nevertheless met squarely and effectively dealt with before the end of the conference.

The press serves also on occasion as an unofficial means of communication between governments, when one party or the other desires for some reason to eschew the usual diplomatic channel. The well-known Balfour note of August 1, 1922, on the subject of interallied debts, contained a statement that when the loans in question were made the United States "insisted, in substance if not in form, that though our allies were to spend the money it was only on our (British) security that they (the United States) were prepared to lend it." On August 24 the Secretary of the Treasury issued a *communiqué* to the press which did not refer specifically to the Balfour note but was generally accepted as in effect a reply to it on the point mentioned. The *communiqué*, which was of course at once cabled to Great Britain by the press, referred to a number of inquiries received as a result of statements recently published with respect to the exact status of the obligations of foreign governments held by the United States and asserted that the statement that the United States Government virtually insisted upon a guarantee by the British Government of amounts advanced to the other Allies was evidently based upon a misapprehension.[10]

This use of the press is unobjectionable in the absence of an unfriendly ulterior motive, but, if not objectionable, then usually unsuccessful at least, when the aim is to reach a people over the shoulders of its government or its plenipotentiaries. Such an attempt formed one aspect of the Genet episode in the early history of the United States. Deforgues, French Minister of Foreign Affairs, wrote Genet a letter of reproof, July 30, 1793, in which he recalled that Genet has been directed "to treat with the Government and not with a portion of the people."[11] The method first took on modern efficiency, however, with the drive led by President Wilson during the World War to set up a difference, in respect to purposes and aspirations, between the German people and the Imperial German Government. Then came the Fiume incident at the Peace Conference, when on April 23, 1919, President Wilson permitted the publication in the press of a statement which was intended, according to Mr. Lansing, "as an appeal to the people of Italy to abandon the claim to Fiume and to reject their Government's policy of insisting on an unjust settlement." In a public reply on the following day Signor Orlando said that "the practice of addressing nations directly constitutes surely an innovation in international relations." "If these appeals," he continued, "are to be considered as addressed to nations outside of the Governments which

[10] New York *Times*, Aug. 2, 3, and 25, 1922.
[11] Sorel: *L'Europe et la revolution française*, 3: 431.

represent them (I might say even against the Governments), I should feel deep regret in recalling that this process, heretofore applied to enemy Governments, is today applied for the first time to a Government which has been and intends to remain a loyal ally of the great American Republic, namely, the Italian Government. . . . To place the Italian people in opposition to the government would be to admit that this great free nation would submit to the yoke of a will other than its own, and I should be forced to protest strongly against suppositions unjustly offensive to my country." Mr. Lansing records that a tempest of popular fury against President Wilson swept over Italy from end to end and that from the most revered of all men by the Italians he became the most detested.[12]

[12] Lansing: *The peace negotiations*, p. 232. For Orlando's statement see *Current History* (June, 1919), 10: Pt. I: 407-408.

It has been said that in replying January 16, 1863, to an address of the workingmen of Manchester, England, President Lincoln "went over the heads" of the British Foreign Office, but this is not the case. The address of the workingmen was delivered to Charles Francis Adams, the American Minister at London, and by him forwarded to the Department of State. The President's reply was transmitted by Seward to Adams. Seward wrote Adams: "You will judge whether the proprieties of diplomatic relations require that a copy of the address shall be submitted to Her Majesty's Government and if you think it necessary you are authorized informally to confer with Earl Russell on the subject." Adams reported February 12 that he had had a conference with Lord Russell at the Foreign Office and read to him the President's address. Lord Russell "expressed himself gratified with the compliment conveyed in submitting it to him." *Dept. of State MSS. Despatches and Instructions, Great Britain.* See *Diplomatic Correspondence*, 1863, 1: 109, for Adams' despatch of Feb. 12, 1863. For the text of the President's message see Lincoln: *Complete works*, 2: 301.

The maneuver was tried at Lausanne by the Russian Soviet delegation without producing any result, not even a public furore. On December 9, 1922, M. Chicherin, going over the heads of the Turkish delegates, appealed to the Ottoman people, through the Turkish press, to insist on the closing of the Straits to foreign warships and on constructing powerful fortifications along the Dardanelles and Bosphorus to guarantee their national security. The appeal was ignored by the Turkish delegates and received calmly by the Turkish press. One Turkish publicist, cabling to Constantinople, introduced the narrative of Chicherin's warnings by relating the story of the Grand Vizier, who, when in doubt as to how to rule his realm, invariably decided upon a policy the reverse of that desired by Russia.[13]

The routine of diplomatic intercourse has been broken by international conferences as circumstances seemed to require, ever since the gatherings at Osnabrück and Münster in 1648 ushered in, with the Treaty of Westphalia, the modern state system. The close of the Napoleonic wars was marked by an especially important series of conferences, from Châtillon in 1814 to Verona in 1822, and attended variously by the Emperors of Austria and Russia and the governing heads of other states, as well as their plenipotentiaries. Satow lists in all fifty-six international meetings of outstanding importance during the 266 years which bridged the span from Westphalia to the World War.[14]

[13] Washington *Post,* Dec. 10 and 11, 1922.
[14] *Op. cit.,* 2:1-171. Satow endeavors to distinguish between congresses and conferences, but whatever difference may once have existed seems now to have lost its significance.

The impulse given by the World War to the conference method of diplomacy has been much remarked upon. Sir Maurice Hankey testifies to attendance at no less than 488 international meetings from 1914 to 1920. In an article on the subject, contributed to *The Round Table* for March, 1921, he discovers the genesis of "diplomacy by conference," not in the fifty-six congresses and conferences listed by Satow, but in the pre-war development of the conference method within the British Empire, leading to the formation of the Committee of Imperial Defense in 1911. This may be not without reason, for the meetings during the World War, which Sir Maurice attended as Mr. Lloyd George's lieutenant, were essentially military in purpose rather than diplomatic, though the extension of military effort to include every department of national life brought all subjects within their purview and called for the leadership and authority of the responsible political heads of governments instead of military commanders only. Technical military conferences were tried at first, but, Hankey recounts, a meeting of the heads of governments was called July 6, 1915, at Calais after France and Great Britain had learned "the overwhelming difficulty of concerting their policy, through the ordinary diplomatic channels, when so many factors entered into the situation." The bringing together of the responsible heads and fountains of authority in secret and informal deliberation proved a great advantage. Hankey relates that the Rome Conference of Christmas, 1916, at which the diplomatic task of drafting the allied reply to the German peace note was accomplished, was at first much too large for the transaction of any real business and secrecy was impossible. Before long the principals adjourned to an inner room at the Consulta, where the formality which had been creeping over the larger gathering was cast aside; and the discussions took place in an atmosphere of intimacy and the greatest good humor.

These swift and secret methods were attuned to war and necessary to its practical success. When peace was to be written, the situation changed fundamentally. The problem was no longer primarily military but political, *i.e.*, diplomatic. The same men, however, remained at the head of the principal allied governments, and they carried into the Peace Conference some of the methods to which the exigencies of war had accustomed them. Hankey records that after the return to Paris in March, 1919, of Lloyd George and Wilson, the Council of Ten continued to function for a few more meetings, but progress was slow. Really intimate discussions became more and more difficult. Above all, Hankey says, a most irritating leakage commenced. The views expressed by members were repeated outside and published often in a perverted and exaggerated form. Eventually the principals surmounted the difficulty by withdrawing to a smaller room, establishing thereby the Council of Four. The Council of Ten did not absolutely come to an end, but henceforth it met less often. The principal conclusions of the German treaty were reached by the Council of Four.

It may be safely said, without attempting in any way an appraisal of the work of the allied statesmen at Paris, that the mode of procedure described by Sir Maurice Hankey accounts in some measure for the criticism which the proceedings of the conference aroused.[15] If the wartime thought of coördinating military effort against a common enemy could have given way to the political conception of establishing a durable peace, the methods of the conference might have been different; and the conference might have taken its place in the succession of world meetings as that which reflected in its most advanced form the democratic spirit of the times. As it was, the enthusiasm for democracy which was generated in the struggle against Germany had to await diplomatic fruition in the Washington Armament Conference two years later. The Washington Conference, both in respect to the character and extent of the publicity given to its proceedings and in regard to special features, such as the assignment to the American delegation of an advisory group fully representative of the nation, stood in some contrast to the procedure at Paris, and marks no doubt the furthest advance today in democratic diplomacy.

Owing in part to the success of the Washington meeting, the idea of diplomacy by conference has gained a wide appeal. The practical advantages of getting a variety of legs under one table have taken hold on the public imagination, especially in the United States and Great Britain. Yet it is recognized by the better informed that an international conference is by no means the solvent of every situation. Experience has taught that there must be careful diplomatic preparation and conference suggested only when the elements of agreement and a spirit of mutual conciliation have been revealed. The declara-

[15] *Cf.* Baker: *Woodrow Wilson and the world settlement,* 1: 139.

tion before the Moscow Soviet last May, credited by the press to Chicherin, that "Russia will not go back a single step before the (British) demands; we, therefore, offer a conference," was exquisitely humorous, though probably not intended to be so. A member of the House of Lords, criticizing the Genoa Conference for the lack of advance preparation, recalled the following statement by Lord Odo Russell, the British Ambassador to Berlin, during the preliminaries of the Berlin Congress of 1878: "Our view as to the congress is that, though it is an admirable instrument to enable friendly powers to come to an agreement about details, it only aggravates the divergence between those who radically differ, because it accentuates and calls public attention to the amount of difference and makes retreat on either side a loss of honor."[16]

"Details" is too strong a word, and there may have been too much "advance preparation" for the Congress of Berlin, but the thought is the same which American statesmen[17] have recently had to emphasize in restraint of undiscriminating demands for "a conference" whenever the international situation becomes particularly exigent. The nature, advantages, and limitations of "diplomacy by conference" were suggested by Mr. Hughes in an address delivered May 18, 1922, before the Chamber of Commerce of the United States, when he said:

[16] *Parliamentary Debates, Lords,* 5th series, 51:15.
[17] See, *inter alia,* speech by Senator Hiram Johnson in *Cong. Rec.,* Jan. 9, 1923, p. 1471, and address by Senator Pepper before the New York State Bar Association as reported in the New York *Times,* Jan. 20, 1923.

"Everyone familiar with foreign affairs knows that while the statement of foreign policies in formal writings is absolutely necessary, still in order to accomplish results in negotiations, there should be so far as practicable the personal contacts of diplomatic representatives. . . . An hour of direct intercourse between responsible Ministers is often worth months of written communications. The international conference itself is largely successful in inverse proportion to its numbers and to the extent that it represents the common purpose of a few who are interested in a particular problem and sincerely wish to find an appropriate method of solution. In the larger gatherings real accomplishment is likely to be hindered by the breaking up into groups with rival purposes which prevent results. The point is that the present effort of diplomacy is not to rely on mechanical facilities of communication but to get to the maximum the advantage of personality in negotiations. The method of conference is a mere extension to a group of that which in a limited way is found every day in the contacts of public ministers representing their different countries."

When the mind turns back from the Washington Conference to the cynical immorality and corrupt methods of the diplomacy of the seventeenth and eighteenth centuries and passes in historical review the development of the instrumentalities and processes of international intercourse from that time until the present, the salient fact emerges—perhaps contrary to the general belief—that, while deep principles rooted in human nature remain the same, the methods of diplomacy are always in the making. Its rules are not fixed[18] but are evolved in practice and correspond to the circumstances, character, and requirements of each generation. Diplomatic processes were soon adjusted to the changes wrought by the reduction of time and space through science, and they are yielding now to the exigencies of a widening public interest. "Diplomatic practice," wrote Pradier-Fodéré in 1881 in the introduction to his *Cours de Droit Diplomatique,* "is of all branches of political science that which is influenced the most by the advances made in social customs, public thought and institutions. The usages, the forms, the rules of which it is made up vary less with countries than with the times and its character changes ceaselessly according to the modifications introduced into the political and social state of the nations."

[18] The rules adopted at the Congress of Vienna (1815) and Aix-la-Chapelle (1818) and subsequently acceded to by the Powers generally relate only to matters of rank and precedence. Satow, *op. cit.,* 1: 235-236; Moore's *Digest,* 4: 430.

CHAPTER III

NATIONAL ORGANIZATION—EUROPEAN DEMOCRACIES

In the last meeting we discussed the instrumentalities and processes of international intercourse from an international or world point of view. Our next step is to examine, from the point of view of constitutional law, the organization maintained for the purpose of international intercourse by the individual states. We shall sketch in, first, constitutional background and then touch upon administrative organization with particular reference to recent measures of reform.

CONSTITUTIONAL BACKGROUND

As forecast in our previous discussion, there are in the constitutional provisions of democratic states relating to the conduct of foreign affairs certain fundamental uniformities, which correspond, it may be presumed, on the one hand, to the influence of the democratic principle and, on the other, to the practical exigencies of international intercourse under the existing organization of international society. These may be stated as follows, in the order of their normal historical development. First, the initiation and pursuit of foreign policy are entrusted to the executive branch of government. Secondly, the legislature participates in the conclusion or enforcement of international acts which have the nature or effect of domestic legislation.[1] Thirdly, the legislature

[1] The principle that the legislature should participate in the conclusion or enforcement of international acts having the nature

exercises some degree of control over the general course of foreign policy. The differences among particular constitutions of the modern democratic type are found chiefly in the relative weight attaching to these elements. Historical precedent for the most part would vest the conduct of foreign relations exclusively in the executive. The modern democratic tendency emphasizes the rôle of the legislature, but holds to the practical necessity of allowing the executive as free a hand as possible in a world of conflicting national interests.

Gradual displacement of the old by the new may

or effect of domestic legislation has not been applied scientifically. It may even have been applied unconsciously in some cases. It is noted that not all treaties which might be considered to have this character are included in the specific enumerations of treaties requiring legislative sanction found in various constitutions, while, on the other hand, these enumerations embrace treaties which do not fall clearly within the category indicated but are of vital importance to the state. The French constitution mentions, for example, treaties of peace. Such treaties may contain particular provisions having the nature or effect of domestic legislation, but they were probably not mentioned in the French constitution on that account but rather because of their vital importance. See on this point Michon: *Les traités internationaux devant les chambres*, p. 252. A clearer example is found in the Spanish constitution, which requires special authorization by law for the ratification of treaties, among others, of "offensive alliance." Nevertheless, it is believed that the principle which historically first led to limitation upon the treaty-making power of the executive has been that stated, namely, the inconsistency of excluding the legislature from participating in what is effectively domestic legislation, and it is from this basis that general legislative control is being extended over the whole domain of foreign policy. Article 68 of the Latvian constitution reads: "The ratification of the Saeima shall be indispensable to all international agreements dealing with questions to be settled by legislative measures."

be observed in the theory and practice of the British constitution. The conduct of foreign relations remains in theory a royal prerogative. The Crown "represents the empire in all external relations, and in all dealings with foreign powers. It has power to declare war, make peace, and conclude treaties." The participation of Parliament in acts having the nature or effect of domestic legislation has come to be assured, however, by the establishment of the constitutional principle that "without the sanction of Parliament, a treaty cannot impose a charge upon the people, or change the law of the land, and it is doubtful how far without that sanction private rights can be sacrificed or territory ceded."[2] Finally, Parliament has come to exercise control over the general course of foreign policy by control of the purse and by the general development of parliamentary authority and ministerial responsibility. The effectiveness of parliamentary authority is derived from the fact that the prerogatives of the Crown are exercised through ministers who are responsible not to the Crown but to Parliament for the Crown's public acts. Actual authority for the conduct of foreign relations vests, accordingly, not in the Crown, but in the Foreign Secretary or in the Cabinet, who are answerable at all times in all matters to Parliament.

It may be noted that the personal influence of the sovereign is greater in the field of foreign relations than in that of domestic legislation, becoming at moments even decisive when the sovereign for the time being evinces special ability in this regard and

[2] Lowell: *The government of England,* 1: 22.

a disposition to interfere.[3] It should also be noted that the Foreign Secretary, in the exercise of his functions, is subject in a special degree to the supervision of the Prime Minister and that of his other colleagues in the cabinet. "We have already seen," writes Lowell, "that every despatch of importance ought to be submitted, before it is sent off, both to the Prime Minister and to the sovereign; and, as a rule, the telegrams, together with correspondence of peculiar interest, are also circulated among all members of the cabinet. In fact there is probably no department where the executive action of the minister is so constantly brought to the notice of his colleagues."[4] The situation was disclosed by Sir Edward Grey when he said in the course of a speech in 1912: "A considerable amount of fault has been found with what some people think is and what they call my foreign policy, but which, of course, ought not to be called my foreign policy because it is quite impossible for any individual Foreign Minister to carry out a policy which is not also, in its main lines, the policy of the Cabinet of which he is a member."[5] Mr. Lloyd George has demonstrated that a Prime Minister may practically supersede the Foreign Secretary in the actual conduct of foreign affairs.

In the course of the past half-century two unsuc-

[3] Lowell, *op. cit.*, 1: 41-45. There is an interesting discussion of the rôles of Victoria, Edward VII, and George V in McBain and Rogers: *The new constitutions of Europe*, pp. 140-146.

[4] Lowell, *op. cit.*, 1: 69 and 88.

[5] Cited in Myers: *Legislatures and foreign relations*, in *Am. Pol. Sci. Rev.*, 11: 668 (Nov., 1917). As to the existence of a similar situation in France, see Barthélemy: *Démocratie et la politique étrangère*, p. 159.

cessful attempts have been made to reinforce by concrete enactments the authority of Parliament. In 1886 a motion was made in the House of Commons to the following effect: "That in the opinion of this House, it is not just or expedient to embark in war, contract engagements involving grave responsibilities for the nation, and add territories to the Empire without the knowledge and consent of Parliament." The motion was lost, though only by four votes, apparently for the reasons fundamentally that the proposed control was felt to be impracticable and that the workings of parliamentary government and ministerial responsibility were deemed to keep the executive normally in agreement with the sense of the country in respect to foreign affairs.[6]

In the midst of the war, March, 1918, it was moved that "in the opinion of this House, a standing committee of foreign affairs should be appointed, representative of all parties and groups in the House, in order that a regular channel of communication may be established between the Foreign Secretary and the House of Commons which will afford him frequent opportunities of giving information on questions of foreign policy and which, by allowing members to acquaint themselves more fully with current international problems, will enable this House to exercise closer supervision over the general conduct of foreign affairs." Four hours of debate ensued. The motion was supported by a number of Liberal and Labor members on the ground that the proposed committee would tend to do away with secret diplomacy, bring the conduct of foreign relations more

[6] Hansard, 3d series, 303: 1386-1422. See especially Mr. Gladstone's speech at p. 1400 and Mr. Bryce's at p. 1420.

effectively into the control of Parliament and the people, and strengthen the hand of foreign secretaries by assuring them of parliamentary and popular support. The argument for the Government was made by Mr. Balfour. He deemed the proposal neither practicable nor democratic. A standing committee of this character would not accord with the workings of parliamentary government; it would hamper the executive and by introducing indirection lessen rather than increase the effective control of Parliament.[7]

The motion was voted down by acclamation in a depleted House, but even among the members who supported Mr. Balfour's view a feeling was noticeable that in the years just preceding the war neither Parliament nor the country had been taken sufficiently into the confidence of the Foreign Secretary. Since the war there has been a persistent demand that Parliament should be currently consulted with regard to questions of foreign policy, and there seems to have been a corresponding readiness on the part of the Government to consult Parliament. Certainly there has been no lack of parliamentary discussion of the situation in the Ruhr. It still remains difficult to determine just what progress is being made in respect to the constitutional authority of Parliament. After the Paris Peace Conference a bill was introduced "for carrying into effect the treaty of peace between His Majesty and certain other

[7] *Parliamentary Debates, Commons,* 5th series, 104: 841-902. For early discussions of the project for a foreign affairs committee see Low, Sidney: *Foreign office autocracy,* in *Fortnightly Review* for Jan., 1912, and Morrell, P.: *The control of foreign affairs,* in *Contemporary Review* for Nov., 1912.

Powers," but this may not have gone beyond the constitutional rules already noted. The proposed Anglo-American guarantee to France contained an explicit provision that it should not become binding until approved by Parliament, but it has been suggested that this was an evidence of Mr. Lloyd George's desire to avoid responsibility rather than a recognition of Parliament's constitutional right.[8]

While the development in this respect remains uncertain, another change is in progress. The successful assertion by the self-governing Dominions of a right to participate in the conduct of imperial foreign relations has been so rapid since the war as to be hardly short of revolutionary. Three important precedents have been established. First, it has become customary for Dominion statesmen to meet with those of the United Kingdom for the purpose of formulating policy. Such a meeting held at London in June, 1921, reviewed the question of the Anglo-Japanese Alliance and took decisions leading to the acceptance by the British Empire of the invitation of the United States to the Conference on Limitation of Armament and Far Eastern Questions. Secondly, the inclusion of representatives of the Dominions, as such, in British plenipotentiary delegations has been established at the Peace Conference in Paris and confirmed at Washington. Thirdly, the Treaty of Peace has been debated and approved by each Dominion Parliament and has been ratified for it, not on the advice and responsibility of the Government of the United Kingdom, but on the advice and responsibility of the Dominion Government con-

[8] *Cf.* McBain and Rogers, pp. 147-148, and Chow: *Contrôle parlementaire de la politique étrangère*, p. 62.

cerned. The treaties resulting from the Washington Conference have been subject to ratification by the Dominion Parliaments. These are plain constitutional precedents which lay down a broad basis of democratic control by assuring not only the participation of Dominion legislatures in the ratification of international acts of imperial scope but also the exercise by these legislatures, through their respective ministers, of a part in the initial formulation and subsequent pursuit of imperial foreign policy.[9]

French constitutional development, stormier and more radical than that of Great Britain, has shifted the weight of authority in the field of foreign affairs further in the direction of the legislature. The constitution of 1875 provides (Article 8) that the President of the Republic shall negotiate and ratify treaties which he shall notify to the Chambers "as soon as the interest and security of the State permit;" but the right of the legislature to participate in acts having the nature or effect of domestic legislation is explicitly secured by the further provision that "treaties of peace, of commerce, treaties which engage the finances of the state, those which are relative to the status of persons and to the right of property of Frenchmen abroad, are definitive only after having been voted by the two Chambers," and

[9] Lewis, M. M.: *The International status of the British self-governing Dominions*, in the *British Yearbook of International Law*, 1922-1923, and Dennis, A. L. P.: *British foreign policy and the Dominions*, in *Am. Pol. Sci. Rev.*, Nov., 1922. The situation is not defined in many respects. The Imperial Conference which is to take place at London during October, 1923, may bring some interesting decisions.

that "no cession, no exchange, no annexation of territory may take place except by virtue of a law."

"One might be tempted to believe," writes a French authority, "that this enumeration is so comprehensive that it submits to the direct collaboration of Parliament all of foreign policy. Because they have limited themselves to a study of the text, in a strictly juridical spirit, certain authors have perhaps exaggerated in this way the effect of the enumeration. 'It would have been simpler,' says one of them, 'to stipulate that all treaties should be submitted to the approbation of the Chambers.' Simpler without doubt, but certainly very different. . . . Almost all the great international acts which have marked the course of our foreign policy during a half century, almost all those which have exercised a decisive influence on the destinies of France are the work of the government alone and have been ratified by the President of the Republic on his sole authority. The fact is that Article 8 of the law of July 16, 1875, does not subject to parliamentary approbation the most important perhaps of all treaties, the great political treaties and the treaties of alliance.''[10]

The control which the Chambers may exercise over the general course of foreign policy rests upon a further constitutional provision (Article 9) that the President may not declare war without the assent of the two Chambers, but, as in the case of Great Britain, derives its force more especially from the general operation of parliamentary government. The powers of the President are exercised by or through his ministers, who are responsible to the Chambers, not to him, for executive acts done. While

[10] Barthélemy, *op. cit.*, p. 109.

the personal influence of the President may be greater in foreign than in domestic affairs, it does not appear that in the former field it is comparable to that which may be exercised by British sovereigns. One student mentions the "complete impotency" of the President as one of the chief weaknesses of French foreign policy.[11]

The control of the French legislature over foreign policy is reinforced by a system of committees, which is highly developed, and, according to Bryce, tends in general to lessen ministerial authority and to invest the Chambers with an immediate direction over the whole field of administration.[12] Foreign affairs were dealt with in the Chamber of Deputies by a Committee of Foreign and Colonial Affairs up to 1920. Incident to a general increase in the number of committees, effected in that year, this was replaced by a Committee of Foreign Affairs only. The members of the new committee are chosen by the Chamber annually, instead of every four years as was previously the case. There was no standing committee on foreign affairs in the Senate before the war, but in 1915 one was created for the duration of hostilities and became permanent in 1920. It consists of 36 members and is charged with the examination of questions relating to foreign policy and especially the execution of the treaties of peace. The committee of the Chamber of Deputies may summon before it any persons whose evidence may be required, but when these persons hold an official post,

[11] Stuart, Graham H.: *French foreign policy*, p. 374; see also Bryce: *Modern democracies*, 1: 229; Chow, *op. cit.*, p. 125, and Barthélemy, *op. cit.*, 144-153.
[12] *Modern democracies*, 1: 246.

the minister concerned must first give his consent, with or without the condition that professional secrecy is to be observed. A minister himself may be requested to appear and give explanations to the committee on points of policy, but it is not certain that a minister may be compelled to do so.[13] In certain cases the Committee of Foreign Affairs may be invested by the Chamber of Deputies with the powers of a special commission of inquiry, including the right to hear sworn witnesses and to pursue investigations in any part of France or even abroad. The General Budget Committee of the Chamber of Deputies, which is the most important of all the parliamentary committees, examines the budget for foreign affairs and discusses the yearly credits for that department. It appoints a reporter for this purpose, who comes necessarily into close touch with the Minister, and the report of the Budget Committee on foreign affairs is considered to be a valuable annual record of French policy.

The German constitution of August 11, 1919, provides for a permanent committee of foreign affairs (Article 35), which surpasses its French prototype in that it continues to function in the interims of parliamentary sessions. "Its purpose," according

[13] In February, 1923, M. Poincaré declined, according to a press report, to appear before the Foreign Affairs Committee to explain the situation in the Near East, but subsequently decided to comply with the Committee's request, saying that he would confine himself to setting forth the position as it concerned the different points on which the Committee might ask information, and would refuse any discussion and even reserve the right to decline to answer questions if he judged them inopportune. Associated Press despatch from Paris in New York *Times*, Feb. 10, 1923.

to a French commentator, "is to subject the foreign policy of the government to the constant supervision of the popular representation."[14] It is said that when the project of the constitution was under discussion serious objections were made. The committee would constitute, it was particularly argued, a sort of advance manifestation of distrust in the government, while the control it might exercise would hamper the pursuit of foreign policy. It was answered that in countries where such committees have been created unfavorable results had not been observed. "Moreover," our French commentator adds, "the committee in question need not be primarily a committee of supervision but a means which, in connection with foreign policy, will bring the influence of politically experienced personalities of the Reichstag to bear upon the professional agencies of the diplomatic service." I am informed by a personal friend in Berlin that the committee has remained in session during parliamentary recesses and has exercised a certain influence over the policies proposed by the Ministry of Foreign Affairs, though less than was expected and mostly in secondary matters and in a restrictive or negative direction. The chief obstacle to fuller coöperation with the Foreign Ministry, according to this information, has been the leakage of confidential matter, especially through the Communist members of the committee.

Sweden created through constitutional amendments in 1921 a parliamentary committee of foreign affairs which is not so much a legislative committee

[14] Brunet: *La constitution allemande du 11 août 1919* (Paris, 1921), p. 177.

in the ordinary sense as a confidential advisory council for the executive, made up of members of the legislature. There was provision in the Swedish constitution long ago for a secret parliamentary committee to advise the King at his request upon questions of foreign policy, but it had nearly ceased to exist, having met only twice in the period 1854-1914. The new committee is the result of a demand after the war for broadened democratic control of foreign relations. It is chosen by the two chambers according to a proportional method of representation of the different political parties. It may be summoned by the King "as frequently as matters demand it," or it must be summoned if six members of the committee apply to the Minister of Foreign Affairs for a conference on a stated question. These further stipulations of the constitution are interesting:

In all foreign affairs of importance a conference of this committee for Foreign Affairs ought to take place before arriving at a decision. When a matter is taken up for discussion all accessible information and documents are to be given in and communicated. The decisions arrived at by the King in matters that have been the subject of discussion with the Committee are to be communicated to its members not later than at their next meeting.

At the beginning of each parliament, and subsequently as often as circumstances demand it, the Minister of Foreign Affairs shall give the Committee an account of the general condition of foreign politics that may be of importance to the State.

The members of the Committee ought to show the greatest caution with regard to communicating to others what has occurred at the meetings of the Committee. In cases when the King, or the person presiding over the proceedings in his absence, finds it necessary to exact a pledge of unconditional secrecy, the members are to be bound by this. When a member first takes part in a meeting he shall give a declaration that he will observe secrecy.[15]

I am informed that the committee meets maybe four or five times a year. There was recently a meeting on Russian affairs while Parliament was in recess. It is said that the committee listens to the expositions of the Foreign Minister without extensive comment and that the meetings are chiefly useful to the Minister for the moral support which he derives from them.

The French constitutional arrangements for the conduct of foreign affairs typify the prevailing continental system. War and revolution have destroyed the autocratic structures of Austria-Hungary, Germany, and Russia, and the new constitutions (except Russia) have established parliamentary régimes which approximate the French model.[16] These new constitutions, except in the case of Germany, have not, however, set up parliamentary committees especially devoted to foreign affairs,

[15] Brusewitz: *Parliamentary control of foreign affairs in Sweden,* in *Foreign Affairs* (London), Jan., 1922. During the war a special consultative parliamentary committee was maintained in Norway. It was composed of representatives of all political parties and is said to have met frequently with the Minister of Foreign Affairs. Pedersen: *Foreign policy control in Norway,* in *Foreign Affairs* (London), Dec., 1921.

[16] See reports submitted in 1911 by the British diplomatic missions and printed in *Command Papers* for 1912, Miscellaneous No. 5, *Treatment of international questions by parliaments in European countries, the United States and Japan;* and McBain and Rogers, *op. cit.,* p. 150. The texts of the constitutions of Latvia and Lithuania, which are not included in the latter work, may be found in *Current History* for December, 1922.

though provision has been made in a number of cases for general parliamentary committees of control to sit during the parliamentary recesses, and it may be assumed that these will have some competence in respect to foreign affairs. It must be said, however, that the striking feature of the new constitutions is their apparent failure to contribute anything essentially new to the solution of the problem of democratic control of foreign affairs, which is, indeed, according to Bryce, one of the most difficult, if not insoluble, problems of practical politics. The Esthonian and Latvian constitutions, which provide for plebiscites, expressly except foreign affairs from their operation. Popular referendum for treaties was added to the Swiss constitution in January, 1921, and this we shall discuss at a later session; but, with that exception, no wholly new constitutional expedients for the democratization of the conduct of foreign affairs have been born in the midst of all the constitution-making which has followed the war. The livelier concern in international relations which the war has imparted to the individual citizen is finding its chief expression in extra-constitutional channels and by an enlarged or more forceful use of existing constitutional implements.

ADMINISTRATIVE ORGANIZATION

The concrete results of a greater popular interest may be observed in the field of administrative organization, in the reform of foreign offices and foreign services. The countries in which such reforms have been accomplished on an important scale include Great Britain, France, Italy, Belgium, the Netherlands, Norway, Sweden, Denmark, and the

Argentine. Two main impulses seem to have been present. The first was a desire to hasten economic recuperation after the war by providing the most effective governmental support for private enterprise abroad. The renewal of a condition of comparatively free competition was looked to with apprehension after the state socialism of the war, and all feared to be behindhand. The second impulse was to democratize and at the same time to vitalize and improve the instrumentalities of diplomacy, which in the pre-war period of comparative public indifference to foreign affairs seemed in some measure to have got apart from the fresher currents of public life.

Naturally enough the first impulse was felt strongly in Great Britain. As early as 1917 the Department of Overseas Trade was created with a view to encouraging and supporting British private enterprise in foreign fields. There had been conflicts of effort and authority between the earlier and uncoordinated instrumentalities for this purpose, the Foreign Office and the Board of Trade. The Department of Overseas Trade was given control and direction of the commercial intelligence work of the Consular Service and of a newly created Commercial Diplomatic Service. Its principal officer was made an Under Secretary in both the Foreign Office and the Board of Trade, and his organization was subordinated to those two ministries. The arrangement was apparently a result of compromise and was not wholly satisfactory to anyone. Sir Arthur Steel-Maitland, the first head of the Department, resigned on account of the difficulties of his position. It is said that the Department has since gravitated rather in the direction of the Foreign Office and collaborates closely with it in directing the trade work of consuls and of the new commercial diplomats.

The Commercial Diplomatic Service, the second result of the British desire to foster a restored commerce, was made to consist of two grades of officers, Commercial Counsellors and Commercial Secretaries. These officers are attached to the British diplomatic missions abroad and their duties are to look after British economic interests generally and to coördinate in each country the local efforts of consuls in that direction. The 1923 *Foreign Office List* shows five Commercial Counsellors and thirty Commercial Secretaries.

The progress of French reform in the interest of trade was not essentially different from that in Great Britain. The National Bureau of Foreign Commerce, formerly only a semi-official organ in the Ministry of Commerce and Industry, was given full official standing. This Bureau, which was first organized in 1898 under the auspices of the Chamber of Commerce of Paris, now serves as a direct medium of communication between French merchants and manufacturers on the one hand and foreign markets on the other. There is a Council of Administration chosen by various agencies, among which the chambers of commerce figure prominently. Contact with the foreign field is maintained through French diplomatic and consular representatives and new commercial representatives similar to the commercial diplomats of Great Britain.

The close association of official effort with private enterprise is exemplified also in the Danish reforms—to mention only one other country. A Trade

Information Bureau was created as an integral part of the Foreign Ministry. This bureau is headed by a practical business man who acts in conjunction with a council made up of representatives of the more important trades and industries of the country and of the Ministries of Commerce and Agriculture. At the same time the organization of the Danish Foreign Service was modernized.

Measures of this character intended to give effective governmental support to foreign trade were accompanied by, and mingled with, measures responsive more directly to the impulse to democratize and vitalize diplomacy. There was a widespread tendency to remove the barriers between the Diplomatic and Consular Services and in Great Britain between those services and the Foreign Office. The distinction between the Diplomatic and Consular Services was based to a considerable extent upon a distinction between political and economic interests. It became clear that diplomacy could not be kept apart from commerce. Political projects could not be carried forward without regard to commercial interests, nor could commercial interests exist without regard to political conditions. Recognition of these facts opened the way for the consolidation of the diplomatic and consular branches of Foreign Services, and the manifest administrative convenience of the change furthered the movement. Interchangeability between the two branches now exists without restriction in Italy, Belgium, Sweden, and Denmark, while in France and Norway there are only minor limitations relating to certain grades. Individuals may be shifted from consular to diplomatic work, or *vice versa,* as the public interest seems to require. At the same time the interior organization of Foreign Offices tended to change. Bureaus and divisions formerly dealt with diplomatic and consular matters and with political and economic matters as such. The present tendency is to mark out the subdivisions by geographical lines, to apportion the world among half a dozen or more groups of experts —political, economic, and legal—who deal, under certain special exceptions, with all the matters which arise in the regions of their respective jurisdiction.

The influence of all these measures has been to break down tradition, to do away with encrusted habits of thought which, surviving from an earlier time, had fallen out of tune with democratic philosophy and had led radical thought to look upon diplomacy as an anachronism, outworn, useless, and even harmful. At the same time direct measures of democratization were adopted. These included the granting of more adequate compensation, admission to the services under competitive conditions, and promotion on merit. Candidates for entrance into the British Diplomatic Service were formerly required to possess a private income of not less than £400 a year. The candidate had moreover to be especially nominated by the Foreign Secretary in order to take the entrance examination. These requirements have been done away with. At the same time the salaries and allowances of the various grades have been increased so as to make the Foreign Service more nearly possible to men not of private fortune. Similar measures have been taken in other countries.

These administrative reforms, minor as they may appear in themselves, tend to give a more widely representative character to diplomacy and to attract to the foreign service of their country those of serious intent. They give substance to the thought of Pradier-Fodéré expressed forty years ago, when he wrote: "The object of permanent missions is above all to follow the progress of civilization among the peoples where diplomacy takes up its residence. In our day the diplomat who does not add to the special knowledge which his profession requires an extended acquaintance with all that makes up the wealth, the power, the material and moral progress of the nations will be but a very mediocre agent. The aristocratic societies of the past could get along with clever, brilliant and agreeable diplomats; modern democracy has need of agents who are honest, serious and informed."[17]

[17] *Cours de droit diplomatique,* 1: vi and viii. The data respecting Foreign Service reform are taken mainly from Williams: *Foreign service changes world wide,* in *Am. Consular Bulletin,* May, 1921. See also Grew: *Danish foreign service reorganized, Am. Consular Bulletin,* Oct., 1921.

CHAPTER IV

NATIONAL ORGANIZATION—THE UNITED STATES

The democracies of Europe, which we considered at our last meeting, exemplify the parliamentary form of government. In them the legislative branch alone is chosen directly by the people. The executive, as represented by the ministry or cabinet, is but a committee of the legislature, having no direct popular mandate. It continues in power only so long as it can command the approbation and support of a parliamentary majority. It does not hold office for a fixed term but can be turned out at any moment on any matter. Only thirteen minutes are said to have elapsed between the Carlton Club meeting in October, 1922, at which the Conservative group voted to withdraw support from the Coalition Government, and the arrival of Mr. Lloyd George at Buckingham Palace to tender his resignation to the King.

The United States, on the other hand, exemplifies the congressional or presidential form of government. The executive, represented by the President, is chosen by the people for a fixed term and is responsible to them alone for the proper discharge of his duties. The members of his Cabinet are answerable to him. Neither he nor they can be called to account by Congress, except through the cumbersome and unusual process of impeachment for "high crimes and misdemeanors." Instead of the ministerial responsibility of parliamentary governments we have the checks and balances of a carefully devised distribution of powers.

In surveying the constitutions of Europe, with regard to the conduct of foreign relations, we noted certain fundamental uniformities, corresponding, it was suggested, on the one hand, to the influence of the democratic principle, and, on the other, to the practical exigencies of international intercourse under the existing political organization of the world. We found, first, that the initiation and pursuit of foreign policy are entrusted to the executive; secondly, that the legislature participates in the conclusion or enforcement of international acts which have the nature or effect of domestic legislation; thirdly, that the legislature exercises some degree of control over the general course of foreign policy.

These elements are not so readily discernible in the literal provisions of the Constitution of the United States, but their persistent quality is exemplified in American constitutional practice. Thus, though treaties are made the supreme law of the land, the Constitution contains no explicit provision that those having the nature or effect of domestic legislation should pass through the normal legislative process.[1] This principle, the manifestations of which we have noted in European constitutions, is essentially democratic and was soon embodied in the constitutional law of the United States by judicial

[1] Mathews relates in the *Conduct of American foreign relations* (p. 132) that "an attempt was made near the close of the Convention to associate the House of Representatives in the treaty-making power, on the ground that 'as treaties are to have the operation of laws, they ought to have the sanction of laws also.' This proposal was defeated, however, on the ground that 'the necessity of secrecy in the case of treaties forbade a reference of them to the whole legislature.' Madison also suggested the inconvenience of requiring a legal ratification of treaties of alliance."

interpretation. Decisions of the Supreme Court imposed the condition that no treaty which is not self-executing could be put in effect without the concurrence of the House of Representatives, and the further condition that every treaty, so far as it is a law of the land in distinction from a national obligation, might be repealed by congressional legislation.[2]

The leadership of the American executive in the conduct of foreign affairs also rests as much upon practice as upon the explicit provisions of the Constitution. The American Constitution was the first great experiment in the democratic control of foreign relations. Among the governments of Europe this function of sovereignty had theretofore been an exclusive prerogative of the executive, upon which, in the more advanced countries such as England, the legislative branch had intruded only occasionally.[3] The earlier experience of the framers of the Constitution, as well as the works of government to which they referred, had made plain to them the essentially executive nature of the foreign relations function, but they feared the arbitrary use of this prerogative as exemplified by the European practice of the time, and maintained moreover a great respect for the principle of the separation of powers.[4] In the final draft of the Constitution the executive,

[2] Anderson, C. P.: *Extent and limitations of the treaty-making power*, in *Am. Jour. Int. Law*, 1: 636. See also Corwin: *The President's control of foreign relations*, pp. 92 ff., and Mathews, *op. cit.*, pp. 201 and 211.

[3] *Cf.* Turner, E. R.: *Control of diplomacy*, in *The Nation* for June 8, 1916, pp. 615-617.

[4] *Cf.* Wharton: *Revolutionary diplomatic correspondence of the United States*, 1: 460-461; Wright: *The control of American foreign relations*, pp. 135 and 363; and Mathews, *op. cit.*, pp. 131 and 339.

as represented by the President, was not given expressly the authority to conduct foreign relations. There is merely the general statement that the executive power is vested in the President. The President is named commander-in-chief of the military and naval forces of the United States; he is charged with the faithful execution of the laws; but he is endowed explicitly and exclusively with only one prerogative forming an integral part of the foreign relations power, namely, the reception of ambassadors and other public ministers. The basic function of treaty-making is shared with the Senate, as is also the appointing power, and the power to declare war is entrusted to the whole Congress.

It was perhaps the greater part of the wisdom of the framers of the Constitution that, having set up certain safeguards, they were content to let matters work themselves out. Under the explicit provisions of the Constitution there was certainly much latitude of possible development. It seemed to be the expectation at the time that the Senate as a body would act as an advisory council in the formulation of foreign policy.[5] It was even conceivable, having regard only to the literal provisions of the Constitution, that the Senate or the whole Congress might take the lead in the foreign as well as the domestic field. Practice, however, responded to the exigencies of international intercourse in the world as it is, and actual development was strongly the other way.

Reviewing the course of history in this respect, Professor Quincy Wright, in his recent work, *The Control of American Foreign Relations,* points out

[5] See *Federalist,* No. LXXV; also Mathews, *op. cit.,* p. 133.

that whenever foreign problems have come to the front concentrated authority has been developed to cope with them. In the period from 1789 to 1829, when foreign relations were complex, Presidents were chosen because of their experience in diplomacy, and they displayed competence and leadership. There was friction, Professor Wright relates, but in every case but one[6] the President's policy prevailed. In the period from 1829 to 1898 the problems of the nation were mainly domestic. In these Congress assumed the leadership, and, though Presidents continued to assert their prerogative in foreign affairs, defeats were frequent and the Senate's power of vetoing treaties was strengthened by increased use. Since 1898 a third period has set in, marked by a reassertion of the President's power and influence. There have been conflicts with the Senate, but the initiative of the President in the formulation and pursuit of foreign policy is an accepted fact.[7]

We find then in American constitutional practice the first two conditions which were found to be common also in the constitutional practice of the European democracies. There remains the third point—the control exercised by the legislature over the general course of foreign policy. Here we encounter the distinctive feature of the American system.

Among the European democracies the power of the purse, which is operative also under our constitution,[8] is one source of control, but a more im-

[6] John Quincy Adams' policy with reference to the Panama Congress.
[7] See Corwin, *op. cit.*, p. 126; Wright, *op. cit.*, pp. 149, 335, 360, and 366; and Mathews, *op. cit.*, pp. 4-12 and 339.
[8] See *infra*, pp. 164 ff.

portant source is the direct and daily responsibility of the executive to the legislative branch. This, as we have noted, does not exist in the United States. The substitute, in the conduct of foreign relations, is the constitutional provision that the advice and consent of the Senate shall be necessary to the ratification of all treaties. The exercise of control is entrusted thus to one branch of the legislature and limited to so much of foreign policy as bodies forth in treaty form. The arrangement is characterized further by a special requirement that the consent of the Senate to ratification shall be given only by a two-thirds, instead of a simple, majority.

Much commentary, and some feeling, has been called forth by this arrangement. When Bryce wrote *The American Commonwealth* in the middle eighties he spoke of it in a tone of general approbation. In *Modern Democracies,* written a quarter-century later, he observes that the plan does not work smoothly, adding, however, that neither has any other plan given satisfaction. John Hay, in 1899, smarting under the Senate's repudiation of his treaty with Pauncefote concerning Panama, wrote Choate that "the irreparable mistake of our Constitution puts it into the power of one-third plus one of the Senate to meet with a categorical veto any treaty negotiated by the President, even though it may have the approval of nine-tenths of the people of the nation."[9]

The question takes on at times a burning actuality that is not always conducive to the most sober judg-

[9] Thayer: *John Hay,* 2:219. For Bryce's comments, see *The American Commonwealth,* 1:108-109, and *Modern Democracies,* 2:74 n.

ment. It is interesting to note, apropos of Hay's bitter remark, that his biographer later observes that we can now see that the Senate was wiser than he.[10] The historical fact is that the framers of the Constitution neither anticipated nor desired the conclusion of many treaties. They were willing that the way of a treaty should be difficult. In the Federal Convention Madison observed that it had been too easy in the Continental Congress to make treaties, although the consent of nine states was required for the purpose.[11] A treaty is a vitally important matter. It frequently imposes a limitation upon the sovereignty and independence of the nation. Many feel that a bare majority of the Senate should not, therefore, have its way. A distinguished student of American history recently told me that of important and really desired treaties he could not think of any that had not gone through eventually. In his view the fight in the Senate against the Treaty of Versailles was justified by public opinion.

On the other hand, proposals for constitutional amendments to bring about a more simplified procedure have been put forward from the most respectable quarters, and the case against the present arrangement must be noted. One statement of it, by Mr. Stuart H. Perry, will be found in the *North American Review* of July, 1922. Mr. Perry lays down the thesis that:

> The course of the Senate in disposing of the Four-Power Treaty confirms the conclusion drawn from its treatment of the Versailles Treaty, that the requirement of a two-

---

[10] Thayer, *op. cit.*, 2: 230; see also pp. 226, 240, and 259 ff.
[11] Wright, *op. cit.*, p. 246.

thirds vote combined with the normal operation of party politics has impaired the treaty-making power of this country to a dangerous degree.

Mr. Perry asserts that the motive which prompted the insertion of this provision in the Constitution was, primarily, not to insure that the merits of treaties should be decisively approved, but to appease a demand arising out of the suspicions and jealousies of the states. This particularist sentiment long ago disappeared. Party government has obliterated sectional lines. The Senate has become a body entirely different in character from that which the authors of the Constitution contemplated and stands in a different relationship to the executive. The consideration of treaties instead of being a dispassionate inquiry has become a matter subservient to party policy. Mr. Perry examines in detail the votes on the Versailles and Four-Power Treaties and concludes that the constitutional provision, as modified by political custom, requires in fact a party majority much larger than any administration can ordinarily hope to enjoy. The result is that it is now "impossible for the American Government to do business as effectively as other nations in any matter involving an important treaty."

The difficulty varies naturally with personalities and politics. The matter cannot be safely judged except in broad historical perspective. The most reasonable expectation looks to the assurance of smooth working through constitutional understandings,[12] and the development in this direction is note-

[12] *Cf.* Wright, *op. cit.,* pp. 368 ff.

worthy. As we shall see later,[13] there is frequently informal consultation between the members of the legislative and executive branches. Formal consultation by the President with the Senate may have been discouraged by Washington's experience, but Polk consulted the Senate in advance with respect to the Oregon treaty, and McKinley included leaders from both sides of the Senate in the commission to negotiate peace with Spain. Taking heed from the fate of the Treaty of Versailles and possibly having in mind McKinley's course, Mr. Harding took a further notable step toward coöperation and understanding by including in the American delegation to the Conference on Limitation of Armament the majority and minority leaders of the Senate. Mr. Hughes subsequently testified to the success of the arrangement. In a speech at Boston, October 30, 1922, he said: "At the very outset the President showed at least one way in which cooperation with the Senate could be effected without derogating from executive prerogative. The President chose the majority and minority leaders of the Senate—Senators Lodge and Underwood—as delegates to the Conference, and these leaders were thus in immediate touch with its proceedings. I am happy to say that at no time during the Conference was there any dissension between the delegates. . . . We wrought without partisan motives; there was perfect harmony between ourselves and with the President as we worked together in the interest of our country. The treaties received the assent of the Senate with reasonable promptitude, and this result was a tribute to the wisdom of

[13] *Infra,* pp. 144 ff.

the President in looking to the end from the beginning and in assuring ultimate success by providing for this happy community of endeavor."

In submitting to the Senate, again at the very outset, the question of American participation in the World Court, President Harding took one more step to assure full understanding between the two branches of government, as well as a foreign policy which should be the fruit, after careful deliberation, of the best thought of the nation.

The question remains, To what extent does the veto power of the Senate with respect to treaties give it control over the general course of foreign policy? What important international acts may the President perform entirely on his own responsibility? We have already noted the unqualified authority bestowed upon him by the Constitution to receive ambassadors and other public ministers. He is also given authority to appoint "ambassadors, other public ministers and consuls" of the United States. Normally the concurrence of the Senate is necessary in these appointments and the emoluments can only be provided by the whole Congress; but the authority of the President to appoint "special agents" without senatorial confirmation is well established in precedent, and they may be paid, if the charge is not too great, from the President's contingent fund. The important point, however, is that the initiative rests with the President, and he need not, except within his discretion, receive envoys from, or despatch envoys of the United States to, particular countries. This places in the President's hands the power to grant or withhold recognition of foreign governments.[14] Recent history with respect to Mexico and Russia shows how important an element this power may be in foreign policy.

Secondly, not all international compacts are deemed to be treaties in the sense of the constitutional provision requiring senatorial consent to the ratification. The President may enter into international arrangements by virtue of his powers as Commander-in-Chief of the Army and Navy. The Rush-Bagot agreement for the limitation of naval forces on the Great Lakes originally took such a form, though it was later submitted to the Senate and approved for ratification by the necessary two-thirds majority. From time to time the President has also entered into agreements without the advice and consent of the Senate for the settlement of the pecuniary claims of American citizens against foreign governments. He has authorized also purely diplomatic interchanges which are tantamount to agreements. Such was the exchange of notes which took place with the leading Powers in 1899 and 1900 respecting the "open door" policy in China, the "gentleman's agreement" with regard to Japanese immigration into this country, and the *modus vivendi* with Great Britain, which for a long period after 1885 defined American fishing rights off the coasts of Canada and Newfoundland. There are no fixed criteria to distinguish these agreements from duly ratified treaties. They are more temporary in character as a rule, or they relate strictly to policy and do not demand enforcement by the courts.[15] Note should also be taken

[14] See espc. on these points, Corwin, *op. cit.*, pp. 46-83.
[15] *Ibid.*, pp. 116-125. See also Moore, J. B.: *Treaties and executive agreements,* in *Pol. Sci. Qu.,* 20: 385 (Sept., 1905).

of the power of the executive, exercised in at least one case, to terminate treaties in full form which have been ratified after approval by the Senate.[16]

Finally, though the power to declare war is vested in the whole Congress, the President has much latitude of action with regard to particular situations. He may recognize an existing state of war. He may employ the armed forces of the United States to perform what are technically acts of war in protection of American citizens and rights abroad. One of the most striking examples was the despatch of forces to China in 1900 at the time of the Boxer rebellion. Legislative ratification has generally been given by subsequent treaty arrangements to similar action in the Caribbean region.[17] The President has also what may be termed a negative war power in the function, frequently exercised, of proclaiming the neutrality of the United States when conflicts arise among other powers.[18]

Any of these acts may be an important factor in the determination of the general course of foreign policy. With respect to them the President is free from direct constitutional interference by the legislature, and to that extent the latter is deprived, under the American system, of general constitutional control over the course of foreign policy. The influence which Congress may exercise in practice we shall refer to later when considering the rôle of the

[16] *Cf.* Mathews, *op. cit.,* pp. 225 and 226.
[17] *Cf.* Corwin, *op. cit.,* pp. 126-163.
[18] *Cf.* Mathews, *op. cit.,* pp. 257 and 263. See *ibid.,* p. 336, regarding the President's power to terminate war by presidential proclamation.

legislature as an instrumentality for the crystallization and enforcement of public opinion.

ADMINISTRATIVE ORGANIZATION

Administrative organization for the conduct of foreign affairs has developed slowly in the United States. There has been little public interest in the matter. The Department of State was among the first of the executive departments to be organized and stands at the head of the cabinet list, but it was made a Home Office as well as a Foreign Office and has had to discharge a variety of incidental duties in addition to its more characteristic function.[19] It was more than sixty-five years after the formation of the Government before a law was enacted by Congress giving a semblance of organization to the Foreign Service, and fifty years more before there was any further important legislation on the subject.[20]

The Act of 1856[21] fixed the compensation of diplomatic and consular officers and defined somewhat the duties and accountability of the latter. It was the intention of the framers of that act that it should be the beginning of a permanent consular, and possibly diplomatic, service to be composed of men of experience grown up in the work. To this end provision was made for twenty-five Consular Pupils, who were to be examined before appointment and assigned to consulates in the discretion of the President, but at its next session Congress refused to appropriate the

[19] See Hunt, Gaillard: *The department of state* (New Haven, 1914).

[20] For a full account of the administrative development of the Consular Service up to 1906, see Carr, Wilbur J.: *The American consular service*, in *Am. Jour. Int. Law*, 1: 891.

[21] 11 *Stat. L.* 52.

necessary money for the salaries of these officers and repealed moreover the section authorizing their appointment. Through the persistent efforts of the friends of reform a similar provision was reënacted in 1864. A corps of thirteen Consular Clerks was created. They were to hold office during good behavior and could not be removed except for cause stated in writing and submitted to Congress. This corps, under a somewhat different form, remains in existence today, but it never accomplished its full purpose, chiefly because of the hesitancy of its members to accept promotion to the grades of Consul and Consul General, from which they would be removed at the next turn of the political wheel.

The spoils system continued to dominate the Foreign Service indeed until 1906. An act of that year,[22] drafted by Secretary Root and Senator Lodge, chairman of the Senate Committee on Foreign Relations, perfected the administrative organization of the Consular Service, and provided the basis for an executive order by President Roosevelt establishing a regular system of appointment and promotion. Under this system, which still prevails, original appointments can be made only from among candidates who have successfully passed a very thorough written and oral examination and then only to the lowest grades of the service. Vacancies in the higher posts are filled by promotion. No promotion is made "except for efficiency as shown by the ability of the officer, his promptness, diligence and general conduct and fitness." The political affiliations of candidates are not considered.

[22] 34 *Stat. L.* 99.

This law and the accompanying executive order marked a new era. It is believed that the most potent factor in the movement for reform which had made them possible was a growing public realization that the Consular Service could be instrumental in aiding the development of American export trade. Prior to 1856 there had been published at long intervals compilations of the reports of consuls upon commercial subjects. The law of 1856 authorized annual publication, and in 1880 publication became monthly. Then special reports were issued at more frequent intervals, as the public interest increased, and finally, beginning in 1898, reports of current value were printed daily by the State Department under the title of *Advance Sheets of Consular Reports.* The reproduction of extracts from these reports in the daily press did more perhaps than anything else to arouse that definite interest throughout the country which alone could assure substantial measures of improvement.

This was the period when the United States was first entering the markets of the world on a large scale with products which competed directly with the manufactures of Europe, and American commercial interests became insistent upon the fullest governmental support. The Department of Commerce and Labor was established in 1903, and a separate Department of Commerce a few years later. It was made the particular duty of this new organ to "foster, promote, and develop the foreign and domestic commerce" and industry of the United States. Consular officers were required to prepare and transmit, under the direction of the Secretary of State, such reports as it might call for.[23] This created one of those difficult twilight zones of authority, and it took some years for a system of coördination to be worked out between the new department and the Department of State. The Department of Commerce early began the employment of its own agents in the foreign field in addition to the Consular Service, and in 1915 the office of Commercial Attaché was created.[24] The Commercial Attaché forms part of the American diplomatic mission in the country to which he is sent, being duly accredited by the Secretary of State, but he is appointed by, reports directly to, and receives his instructions from, the Secretary of Commerce. At a recent date some sixteen Commercial Attachés and nine Trade Commissioners were stationed at as many foreign capitals.[25]

After 1856 the Diplomatic Service received no further legislative attention, except the annual appropriations, until 1915. An Act of February 5 of that year, "for the improvement of the Foreign Service,"[26] classified the Secretaries in the Diplomatic Service, and effected an important administrative change by providing that secretaries and consular officers should be appointed and commissioned, not to particular places as theretofore, but to particular

[23] 32 *Stat. L.* 825.
[24] 38 *Stat. L.* 500.
[25] *Commerce Reports,* for Aug. 6, 1923. See also *Tenth Annual Report of the Secretary of Commerce* (1922), pp. 108 ff. For a good account of the situation created by the multiplicity of American official agents operating abroad, see MacClintock, Samuel: *A unified foreign service,* in *Am. Pol. Sci. Rev.,* 16: 600 (Nov., 1922).
[26] 38 *Stat. L.* 805.

grades and should be assigned to posts abroad and transferred from one post to another by order of the President as the public interest might require. Already, by an executive order of November 26, 1909, appointments to, and promotions in, the secretarial grades of the Diplomatic Service had been placed upon a merit basis by provisions similar to those established for the Consular Service three years earlier. In 1911 and at later times the organization of the State Department was altered along the general lines which we have already indicated as underlying Foreign Office reform generally.[27]

There have been no important statutory changes in the organization of the American Foreign Service since the war. The reforms which have been effected by the other leading countries of the world we have already noted. The need of the United States for a modernized and strengthened representation to cope with the multiplied and aggravated problems of foreign politics and to uphold national political and economic interests in a disturbed and somewhat desperate world has not been less than that of other countries, and definite measures have been proposed, though not yet adopted, to meet these requirements of the national interest. The chief deficiencies which are generally deemed to exist at present are (1) absence of organization in the grade of Minister Plenipotentiary, (2) inadequate compensation, (3) rigid separation of the diplomatic and consular branches, and (4) lack of any provision for retirement.

[27] See *supra*, pp. 56 ff. For an account of the development of the so-called geographical divisions in the State Department, see article by Mr. Wm. Phillips, Under Secretary of State, in *Am. Consular Bulletin* for Dec., 1922.

As we have seen, the secretarial grades of the Diplomatic Service have been classified since 1915, and secretaries are appointed to classes and are transferable from post to post as the public interest requires. Ministers and ambassadors, on the other hand, are appointed to particular places; and their whole career is limited more often than not to one place. This is natural enough in the case of ambassadors, who are usually in a special degree the personal representatives of the President, but the grade of minister, it is felt, should, without hampering the President in his free choice of men, be brought within the regular scope of the diplomatic career. It is believed that two desirable results would be obtained in this way. First, the services of trained men for these important posts would be made most readily available to the President and the country; and secondly, a career so rounded out would be most likely to retain the best types developed by actual experience in the lower grades. A bill[28] introduced in the last Congress sought to secure these ends by creating two classes of Minister Plenipotentiary and providing that appointments should thereafter be by commission to one of these classes instead of to a particular foreign capital.

Proposals designed to remedy the other deficiencies noted above are embodied in a separate bill,[29] which bears the name of its sponsor, Mr. John Jacob Rogers of Massachusetts. This bill passed the House in the last Congress by an overwhelming majority and was lost in the Senate only by reason of a filibuster at the close of the session. It will be reintro-

[28] H. R. 10213, 67th Cong., 2d sess.
[29] H. R. 13880, 67th Cong., 4th sess.

duced when Congress convenes in December. The Rogers bill has elicited very wide approval. Mr. Hughes has given it his hearty support. In a letter to the President a year ago he summarized its provisions and what it was expected they would accomplish.

"The main purpose," he wrote,[30] "is to lay the foundation of a broader service of trained men by removing certain embarrassing limitations in the present organization and giving impetus to the idea of diplomacy as a career. This is thought to be necessary as a means of attracting and holding the type of men capable of measuring up to the new demands.

"There are only four important provisions to be considered:

"1. The adoption of a new and uniform salary scale with a view to broadening the field of selection by eliminating the necessity for private incomes and permitting the relative merits of candidates to be adjudged on the basis of ability alone.

"2. The amalgamation of the diplomatic and consular branches into a single foreign service on an interchangeable basis. This would relieve the limitations of the present consular career and effectually coordinate the political and the economic branches of the service.

"3. The granting of representation allowances, which would lessen the demands on the private fortunes of ambassadors and ministers and render it

[30] This letter and other pertinent matter are printed in the report on the bill of the House Committee on Foreign Affairs, House Rpt., No. 1479, 67th Cong., 4th sess. See also the hearings before this Committee on H. R. 12543, Dec. 11-19, 1922.

practicable to promote a greater number of trained officers to those positions.

"4. The extension of the civil service retirement act, with appropriate modifications, to the foreign service. This has become necessary for maintaining the desired standard of efficiency under the merit system.

"Taking up these four points in the order mentioned, it may be further explained that the salaries in both branches of the service, and especially those of diplomatic secretaries, are quite inadequate.

"The present range of consular salaries is from $2,000 to $8,000, with two positions at $12,000; that of diplomatic secretaries from $2,500 to $4,000, whereas the proposed new scale would be subdivided into nine classes, ranging from $3,000 to $9,000. Readjustment on this basis would involve a substantial increase in the salaries of diplomatic secretaries and a smaller increase in consular salaries, requiring additional appropriations as compared with those of the current year of $328,500.

"By assimilating the positions in the Diplomatic Service with the corresponding positions in the Consular Service on the basis of a common salary scale it would become possible through the use of the title 'Foreign Service Officer' as employed in the bill to establish the two branches on an interchangeable basis and secure the highly desirable advantage, from the standpoint of economy and efficiency, of combined administration.

"The principle of providing representation allowances is one which is well established in the practice of other nations and among the important business interests of this country. In relation to the foreign service it is a corollary to the Government ownership of embassy and legation buildings abroad as a means of lightening the burden of personal expense on our ambassadors and ministers. While it is not deemed advisable to request appropriations for this purpose at the present time, I believe it important that statutory provision should be made therefor in order that suitable funds may be provided at a later date and in such proportion as the special exigencies may require.

"Owing to the length of time that the Diplomatic and Consular Services have been on a civil service basis there are a number of positions, especially in the Consular Service, being held by officers advanced in years whose retention impairs the efficiency of the service as a whole. It has become urgently necessary to provide for the retirement of these officers, and in view of the fact that both branches of the service are well established on a civil service basis it appears feasible to bring them under the provisions of the civil service retirement act of May 22, 1920, modified only as to the age of retirement, the rate of contribution, and the rate of annuity. The immediate benefits of such an enactment would be appreciable. In fact, no proposal in connection with the improvement of the foreign service commends itself to my judgment with greater force. The inauguration of the system of retirement upon annuities would entail an initial appropriation of $50,000, but it is estimated that no further appropriation would be required until 1936.

"All the principal nations have reorganized their foreign services since the war. With the comparatively slight but fundamental changes contained in these proposals, which, in fact, represent nothing more than keeping pace with the rapid growth of the present system, I feel sure that a foundation would be laid for a service which would compare favorably with that of any other nation.

"The total additional outlay required for this purpose would be $378,500, of which $328,500 would represent an annual expenditure. This seems to me a small sum when compared with the very substantial improvement in the foreign-service machinery which I am confident would follow the enactment of the proposed measure."

CHAPTER V
INTERNATIONAL ORGANIZATION

TODAY we conclude the first part of our work, namely, the study in its broad outlines of organization and method in international intercourse. We shall then have the necessary background against which to begin, at the next meeting, consideration of the question of the democratic control of foreign relations.

We emphasized at our first meeting the spiritual diversity of the groups or nations into which civilized humanity is divided and the rather bristling individualism of the sovereign states which compose modern international society. It remains now to note the existence of certain international organizations which are the manifestations of an opposite influence, the tendency of the civilized community to draw together in the pursuit of its common interests. These organizations may be classified in a general way as administrative or technical, political, and judicial.

The final dissolution of the Holy Roman Empire in 1806 removed the last vestige of the old order of international society which preceded the present state system. Interestingly enough, the Empire had become, just two years before its disappearance, party to a treaty with France, of August 15, 1804, which created the earliest international administrative commission. Navigation upon the Rhine, which then formed the boundary between France and a number of the German states, had become so precarious and costly, owing to the demands and tolls of the various sovereignties controlling it, that an international arrangement to put an end to the abuse became a necessity. The treaty of 1804 substituted uniform and fixed tolls and regulations and created an administrative commission which, under the name of the Central Rhine Commission, has operated successfully, by virtue of an authority renewed from time to time through further treaties, down to the present time.[1]

During the sixty years following 1804 seven other international administrative bodies were formed. These included the Danube Commission (1856) and the Universal Postal Union (1863). In the next twenty-five years, extending from 1865 to 1890, fifteen more were established, including the Universal Telegraphic Union, the Union for the Protection of Industrial Property, and the Pan-American Union; and from 1890 to 1915 the number was twenty-three, including the Sugar Union, the Institute of Agriculture, and the Wireless Telegraphic Union. The acceleration in later years is notable—an average of one for every nine years in the first period, one for every twenty months in the second, one for every thirteen months in the third. It is estimated that in 1915 about forty-five official international bureaus or commissions were in existence.

A survey shows that the earliest of these bodies were created to deal with questions of international communication. International health and morals and commercial and financial questions came next, followed most recently by scientific matters. The serv-

[1] Sayre: *Experiments in international administration* (New York, 1919), pp. 132 ff.; Treaty of Versailles, arts. 354 ff.

ices performed are mostly those of information. Relatively few of the bureaus or commissions exercise any authority. The subjects dealt with are apparently determined by practical considerations alone. These bodies have come into existence spontaneously and independently and have developed in the same free fashion.[2]

When we come to consider international organizations of a political nature, it is necessary to bear in mind that the established instrumentalities of diplomacy constitute the most important existing international organism. They are worldwide, embracing all sovereign states; activity is incessant and frequently directed to world, as distinguished from purely national, ends. This is sometimes lost sight of, or thought is taken only of the more conspicuous forms of diplomatic consultation and common action, such as the Concert of Europe before the war and latterly the Supreme Council and the Council of Ambassadors at Paris. The fact is that most of the concrete instances of international coöperation—now multitudinous in number—have been first put forward through ordinary diplomatic channels and many of them have been carried to fruition in the same way.

In addition to the organism of diplomacy, the nations now support two concrete organizations of a partly political nature—the Pan-American Union and the League of Nations. As a result of action taken at the First International Conference of American States in 1890, an association was formed

[2] Potter: *An introduction to the study of international organization,* chap. xvii. See p. 270 of this work for a list of official international administrative bureaus.

under the title of the International Union of American Republics. To provide for the prompt collection and distribution of commercial data and information among its members the Commercial Bureau of the American Republics was established at Washington. At subsequent conferences the organization was enlarged and perfected, and in 1910 the former commercial bureau became the Pan-American Union. The work of the Pan-American Union is primarily administrative or technical. Its essential purpose is to foster cultural and economic relations among the twenty-one member republics. Though proposals have been made that it should do so, the Union as such has never entered upon distinctly political matters, such as the settlement of specific international disputes, but it has become the natural meeting ground of Pan-American diplomacy and fosters in this way politic understanding and facilitates political adjustments among particular states.[3]

The League of Nations is primarily political. It was created explicitly for political purposes, and possibly its most conspicuous work has had to do with the adjustment, by direct intervention, of difficulties among its members. At the same time it has been made the centre for a great and diversified international activity of an administrative or technical nature. It remains in the formative stage.

The first international organization of a judicial nature was the Permanent Court of Arbitration created by action of the First Hague Conference in

[3] For a brief authoritative statement of the activities of the Pan-American Union and its historical development, see report of the Director General for the period 1910-1923 (Wash., Govt. Ptg. Office, Jan., 1923).

1899 with a view to regulating and facilitating the pacific settlement of international disputes by arbitration, a process which had been in use since ancient times but which had not theretofore been the subject of general and systematic arrangements among the nations. It was not really a permanent body, despite its name, but consisted only of a large panel of judges from which disputants could make a selection in particular cases. A permanent administrative bureau, however, was established at The Hague under the supervision of the local diplomatic corps, which was named for the purpose a permanent administrative council.

The Second Hague Conference effected certain lesser improvements with respect to the Permanent Court of Arbitration, but did not accept proposals put forward by the American delegation for "a development"—to quote from Mr. Root's instructions to the delegates—"of the Hague Tribunal into a permanent tribunal composed of judges who are judicial officers and nothing else, who are paid adequate salaries, who have no other occupation, and who will devote their entire time to the trial and decision of international causes by judicial methods and under a sense of judicial responsibility." A convention was signed for the creation of an International Prize Court, which in its particular field would have been much more nearly a true court, but this project failed of ultimate realization.

The fruition of the American idea came fourteen years later in the organization of the Permanent Court of International Justice, which embodies very largely the proposals of 1907. The new court is a permanent body, consisting of eleven ordinary and four deputy judges, chosen from among the world's eminent jurists without regard to nationality. They serve for terms of nine years, must devote their whole time to the court, and are eligible for reëlection. The court rests upon a special international agreement, to which nearly all the sovereign states of the world have adhered. The question of the adherence of the United States was recently referred to the Senate by President Harding.[4]

These few facts concerning the progress of international organization in its several fields show how the sovereign states are brought together in the pursuit of their common interests and supplement the ordinary processes of diplomacy by the creation from time to time of special organs designed to serve specific purposes. This growth of international coöperation in special forms is an important manifestation. The ordinary mechanism of diplomacy remains, however, the chief organic connection among the sovereign states and the means whereby the great bulk of international business is accomplished.

It has two striking characteristics—the small cost of its operation and its practicality. Its machinery is the simplest. The basic organization, as we have seen, comprises only fifty-odd foreign ministries and some 1,100 foreign missions, the greater part of which consist, I should say, of not more than a dozen persons each. The cost of maintaining this system is

[4] See espc. address by Mr. Hughes on the Permanent Court of International Justice before the American Society of International Law at Washington, April 27, 1923, published, among other places, in the Proceedings of the 17th annual meeting of that society, p. 75; Hyde: *International law,* 2:129-152; Potter, *op. cit.,* chaps. xiv-xvi.

almost nothing compared with the outlays made by governments in other directions. The total annual appropriations for the maintenance of the American Foreign Service, including the whole State Department—the Department of Peace, as Mr. Hughes likes to call it—is at present less than $10,000,000. The aggregate annual cost of all the foreign services of the world, if it were reckoned up, would fall short of a quarter of a billion. The United States alone spent that much in a few days during the World War. For $10,000,000 it is possible to build one cruiser.

Diplomacy is not less practical than it is economical. There is a traditional belief in its elaborateness, based presumably upon the recollection of a bygone ceremony which reflected the manners of the times. In fact, nothing could be simpler. A minister of foreign affairs for each state, surrounded by the representatives of other states having interests at his capital, does business with them, carefully because enormous interests are involved, but in the same way essentially that business is done among individuals. The intricacies of diplomatic procedure are but a myth which can be dispelled at once by a comparison of its few terms and rules with the elaborate systems which have been built up, under the name of parliamentary law, for the guidance of domestic legislative assemblies.

The practicality of diplomacy holds an assurance for the future. Its organization and methods can be easily molded. The forces of undue conservatism are effective only when shielded by public indifference and then only for a moment. We have seen how closely in all ages diplomacy has reflected the spirit of the times. As we approach the question of the democratic control of foreign relations, there need be no misgiving as to the continued malleability of its institutions. They are simple and practical and will continue, as in the past, to accommodate themselves, promptly and almost imperceptibly, to new conditions as they arise.

PART II
DEMOCRATIC CONTROL OF FOREIGN RELATIONS

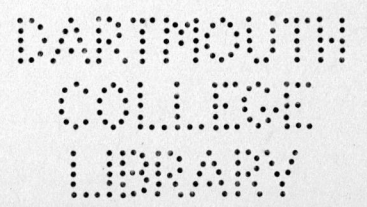

CHAPTER VI

SECRET AND OPEN DIPLOMACY

The first requisite for the democratic control of foreign relations is the dissemination of information among the public. Without information it is plain that there can be no control. "Open diplomacy" has become therefore the shibboleth of democracy in the field of foreign affairs, and our first step must be to consider exactly what it means. Like many watchwords it is used frequently with slight discrimination. The very sibilancy of its antonym, "secret diplomacy," commends it to the undiscriminating as a club wherewith to belabor whatever may displease them in the progress of the world's affairs. In order to arrive at a true definition, it is necessary to distinguish between policy and accomplished facts, on the one hand, and current negotiations, on the other. Open diplomacy rightly understood calls for complete frankness with respect to the first and a maximum of publicity, but not complete publicity, with respect to the second.

FRANKNESS AS TO POLICY AND ACCOMPLISHED FACTS

Formerly the policies of states toward one another were in the nature of things secret. Military conditions alone prevailed in Europe when the Italian cities began at the end of the Middle Ages a systematic diplomatic intercourse, and diplomacy, being but the handmaid of war, shared war's essential secrecy of purpose and operation. This condition of affairs has been modified only with the development of democracy. If the present world system of sovereign states were maintained and each state were a pure monarchy, there would probably be little question of open diplomacy. Each monarch, consulting privately with such counsellors as he might choose, would pursue, according to his nature, a policy of greater or less state selfishness toward all other states. Open diplomacy would supervene only as enlightenment and altruism might grow among rulers.

However, broader repositories of political power have been developed. When through the institution of ministries rulers were placed in commission, examples arose—as recently as that of Napoleon III—of strong-headed or vain monarchs endeavoring by secrecy to hold the play of foreign relationships in their own hands to the exclusion of their ministers; and, since the people have come to be generally recognized as exercising the ultimate sanction of government, we have had instances of monarchs and ministers practicing secrecy as against them. Such was the case of King Carol of Rumania, who concluded successive treaties with the Triple Alliance signed only by himself and his Premier and not communicated to the other members of the Cabinet or to the Chambers, as required by the constitution.

Unconstitutionality is not, however, the more important aspect of secret diplomacy. Its arrangements are usually constitutional enough, and rulers, whether monarchical or democratic, are more often than not honestly devoted to the interests of their people. Certainly this is true of the members of democratic governments. The impulse to secrecy springs as a rule not from a desire to deceive the people but from a supposed imperative necessity to deceive the government of another state. It has its being not so much in undemocratic convictions among statesmen as in state selfishness. If it were possible for a government to apprise its own people of a set of facts without at the same time informing the whole world, the situation would be different. As it is, two diametrically opposed forces operate. One is the normal disposition of political leaders to be honest and take the people into their confidence, if for no other reason than to gain their support. They would often be glad to have political credit for what they have done. The opposite force is a real or supposed public necessity for concealing certain facts from rival states.

The practical influence of these opposed forces depends greatly upon the individual character of statesmen, which is in turn influenced by the character of the times and the people. The general tone of public life has its effect. Secret diplomacy reached a climax at the Congress of Berlin in 1878. The late antagonists settled their differences for a great part in private preliminary negotiations, quietly doublecrossing their late friends. Lord Salisbury concluded a secret arrangement with Russia, and, when news of the agreement was published in a London newspaper before the convening of the Congress, Salisbury asserted in reply to a question in the House of Lords that the statements he had seen were wholly unauthentic and not deserving of confidence. It has been described as "a lie in the grand style." When it subsequently became known that such an agreement had actually been consummated, we are told that public criticism was not directed so much to

Lord Salisbury's evasion as to a contention that too much had been conceded to Russia.[1]

The natural disposition of individual statesmen to tell the people varies not only according to the intensity of the democratic conviction but also with individual temperaments. An outstanding example is that of President Wilson, whose "temperamental limitations" in respect to communicativeness have been remarked upon by his Peace Conference biographer[2] as well as by others. The tradition of diplomacy as a sacrosanct and occult process has also its influence, but this is rather among small and in the long run inconsequential minds. A disposition to be open with the public and gain political support by frequent appeals to popular opinion, is now predominant among the statesmen of the great democracies.

The consideration of public necessity which is sometimes deemed to run counter to the disposition of modern statesmen to be communicative is not to be treated lightly, for it relates to the fundamental right of self-preservation and takes on a moral color. European thought, while generally recognizing secret treaties as undemocratic and undesirable in themselves, is strongly influenced by the struggle for national existence and hesitates to forego any available means of self-defense. Lord Balfour, speaking in the House of Commons in 1918, said: "You cannot lay down, and I do not think you would be wise to lay down, an absolute rule that under no circumstances and for no object, could you so far concede the point as to say that a treaty is to be made

[1] Kennedy: *Old diplomacy and new*, pp. 34 and 35.
[2] Baker: *Woodrow Wilson and the world settlement*, 1: 151.

which is not to become public property. I am perfectly ready to admit that that is not a process which, to me, is a very agreeable one. To reduce secret treaties to the narrowest possible limits should, I think, be the object of every responsible statesman who has the control of foreign affairs. Beyond that I do not feel inclined to go."[3] It is well known that Viscount Grey has been in principle opposed to secret treaties. Just before the war he declined to enter into an engagement of that character with Germany respecting spheres of influence in the Portuguese colonies, unless it should be published along with the earlier secret agreements of 1898 and 1899. "England had as he said"—Prince Lichnowsky relates—"no other secret treaties besides these, and it was contrary to established principles to keep binding agreements secret. Therefore he could not make any agreement without publishing it."[4] Yet Grey acquiesced in the secret treaties of the war, yielding no doubt to what he deemed to be an imperative necessity involving the preservation of the state.

Continental countries do not enjoy England's comparative security from direct military menace. There is an illuminating episode in the history of the French Revolution, described by Sorel in *L'Europe et la revolution française*. The Convention, in March, 1795, decided that the Committee of Public Safety might negotiate treaties of armistice, peace, alliance, and commerce, but these must be confirmed by the

[3] *Parl. Debates, Commons,* 5th series, 104: 878.
[4] Lichnowsky: *My mission to London 1912-1914,* pp. 14 ff. See also Kennedy, *op. cit.,* p. 286 and note.

Assembly. It was then argued that, if the Coalition was to be broken "and the wolves permitted to devour each other," the Government must have the right to enter into secret stipulations. That, the opposition replied, would be to give the Committee *carte blanche* and annul the restrictions theretofore proposed. The argument taking on some heat, Merlin de Thionville declared that "there are none but the enemies of peace who do not wish that there should be secret articles in the treaties." It was pointed out that otherwise separate treaties with the members of the Coalition would be impossible. "I suppose," Boursault observed, "that Austria desires to treat with the Republic, but on condition that the treaty will remain secret for two or three months, because she has herself to treat with another power. If you want this treaty, are you going to divulge this secret, or will you refuse to treat with her on this condition?" The Convention wanted separate treaties and Boursault's argument prevailed. Someone had said: "The French people should treat as the Roman Senate did." "Do we deliberate in the public place?" Cambacérès replied. "Is the Republic made secure by three centuries of victories? You do not sufficiently distinguish between the present time and the time to come. Perhaps then we shall have no other diplomacy than that of Popilius, and that is the diplomacy which I believe worthy of a free people; but we have not yet arrived at that point." The Committee was authorized to conclude secret articles provided that they should have for their purpose "to assure the defense of the Republic and to increase its means of prosperity," and that they should be of a nature neither contrary to nor restrictive of the published articles.[5]

The constitutions of most of the countries of Europe, as we have seen, place it within the power of the executive to conclude secret treaties. The constitutions of the new countries erected since the war are not different.[6] "If we had to seek out," writes a French publicist, "what would be in an ideal world the most perfect of diplomatic systems, one would undoubtedly exclude therefrom secret treaties. But, presented in this way, the question would be nothing but a pure fantasy. The only problem which merits sustained attention is to know, being given the state of the world and particularly of Europe, what system will best enable France to defend her interests therein." "In diplomacy as elsewhere," he adds, "it is necessary to follow the rules of the game. One may be sure that France will not cheat and that she will be unfair toward none; but, in a game where her existence is at stake, she will not have the *naïveté* to show her cards to her adversary."[7]

Possibly it is only with ill grace that Americans, in the security of the western hemisphere, can gainsay this point of view. "I am not unaware," this French publicist observes, "that this sort of political pragmatism shocks a certain number of our

---

[5] Sorel: *L'Europe et la revolution française,* 4: 262 ff.

[6] McBain and Rogers: *The new constitutions of Europe,* p. 150. See also the constitutions of Lithuania and Latvia as printed in the New York *Times Current History* for Dec., 1922. The constitutions of France, except those of 1789-1791 and 1848, have all permitted secret treaties. Barthélemy: *Démocratie et la politique étrangère,* p. 210.

[7] Barthélemy, *op. cit.,* pp. 224 and 227.

friends in the United States of America. They judge us too frequently from the height of their absolute principles. Let them reflect however that they have had until now only a very simple external policy, that they have not had for a long time powerful enemies to fear and that *so far* (1917) they have not felt at their sides a German menace." It would be unintelligent as well as unkind to fail to appreciate the special exigencies which racial crowding and the struggle for existence impose upon national leaders in Europe, but opinion in America, in common with liberal opinion in Europe itself, has been impressed by the unfortunate concomitants of the policies which these leaders seem sometimes to have felt that the situation necessitated. The plea of public necessity, based on the right of self-preservation, is susceptible of dangerous interpretations. The instinct of self-preservation is closely connected with the natural tendency of living organisms, including peoples, to expand, even at the cost of their fellows. To determine where one leaves off and the other begins is frequently difficult, as difficult as to say whether a defensive offensive is justified or who really "struck the first blow"; and it is remarked that some European statesmen, unchecked by public opinion or possibly encouraged by sections of it, have carried the arrangements of secret diplomacy far afield, involving their countries in colonial enterprises particularly which could not be shown to have other than a far-fetched connection with the preservation of the state or the vital interests of the people.

Possibly the severest indictment which secret diplomacy has suffered relates to its connection with the "balance of power." It has been one of the principal methods by which statesmen have pursued that system of policy. It is here that it has its greatest moral justification, coming close to the right of self-preservation, and it is here, according to the liberal view, that it has failed. It is felt that a procedure which is undemocratic, whose only justification is pragmatic, has not in practice succeeded, if one is to count as an essential element of success the maintenance of the general European peace. It seems clear to liberal thought that some of the countries of Europe may have gained temporarily by secret diplomacy, but it is doubted that they gain in the long run. The Triple Entente may have saved Europe from German domination, it is argued, but the Dual Alliance, proceeding by the same method of secret alliance and counter-alliance, missed its goal only by the narrowest margin. It is felt that secret diplomacy tends to defeat its own ends. The existence of secret agreements is usually known, but their extent and character are never certain. Suspicion, fear, bad faith are in turn engendered. There is "insurance" and "reinsurance." Alliances honestly defensive in the beginning take on in time an aggressive character and breed counter-arrangements which pass through the same cycle.[8] A state of mind ensues of which competitive armament is but one symptom and which carries in it the seeds of ultimate disaster.

It was no doubt in this general order of thought that President Wilson in his second inaugural included among the "things we shall stand for" the

[8] *Cf.* introduction to Pribram and Coolidge: *The secret treaties of Austria-Hungary* (Cambridge, 1922).

conviction "that peace cannot securely or justly rest upon an armed balance of power," and placed at the head of his Fourteen Points—

Open covenants of peace, openly arrived at, after which there shall be no private international understanding of any kind but diplomacy shall proceed always frankly and in the public view.

Possibly no other utterance by President Wilson called forth such hearty expressions of approval. In America it was but the statement of an established policy. To Europe it seemed an assurance for the future. The principle of open diplomacy was embodied in the Covenant of the League of Nations, and there was a wide feeling that one evil at least had been done away with. This expectation has not been entirely fulfilled. There was possibly justification in the stress of circumstances for the secret agreements of the war, but it is well known that secret treaties have been concluded since the peace, against which the stipulations of the Covenant of the League have not prevailed. Distinct progress has been made, however. A resolution adopted at the Washington Conference provides for an exchange of texts of existing or future commitments of, or relating to, China. There are peculiar difficulties in the case of China, but the filing of the information is in progress, and it is felt that the moral atmosphere of international relations in that part of the world has been thereby vastly improved. The Prime Minister of England was able to announce in the House of Commons on November 27 last that Great Britain had now no secret treaties. On the continent, where democratic doctrine has been most difficult to apply in practice, the three great autocracies whose methods went far to create those difficulties have been destroyed; and we are still only in the morrow of the war.

PUBLICITY IN THE COURSE OF NEGOTIATIONS

The frequent confusion of thought respecting open diplomacy in its relation to negotiation as distinguished from policy and accomplished facts was strikingly illustrated at the Paris Peace Conference. An important element in what Mr. Ray Stannard Baker describes as the "world over-expectancy" existing at the opening of the Conference was the far-reaching interpretation of President Wilson's first point: "Open covenants of peace openly arrived at." It was assumed, Mr. Baker relates, that this meant that every process at every point would be wide open to public view. The President never meant, he continues, that "the birth pains of the peace" should be utterly exposed, but this explanation, which the President did his best to circulate, never overtook the impression made by his earlier pronouncement. The President later wrote: "When I pronounced for open diplomacy, I meant, not that there should be no private discussions of delicate matters, but that no secret agreements should be entered into, and that all international relations, when fixed, should be open, aboveboard, and explicit." Explaining his views on publicity to Mr. Baker, Mr. Wilson said: "It [the Council] is a kind of world cabinet meeting in which every member may express his views freely. If we announced partial results, or one decision at a time, it might easily result in bloodshed. We must do nothing that will incite more war, we must do everything to get a speedy peace. When we reach real decisions everything must be made known to the world." "At other times the President compared the conferences to the Board of Directors of a corporation or the Executive Committee of a trade union, with private discussions but public decisions."[9]

The matter is indeed not in any way peculiar to diplomacy. As President Lowell brings out clearly in his recent volume, *Public Opinion in War and Peace,* compromise is an ever present and indispensable element in human dealings, and privacy of deliberation is a condition essential to compromise. Unanimous decisions are required from juries; and to that end has been established, President Lowell points out, "a device calculated to prevent jurymen from prematurely making up their minds, and thereby rendering a change of opinion difficult until a final agreement is reached or proves to be unattainable. That is the secrecy of deliberation. Until the jury are discharged their differences are unknown outside their own room, and hence a juryman has little of the pride of opinion which prevents change. When men consult in private and know that they are expected to agree, they are apt to express their views in a tentative way, to heed one another's opinion, to compromise and draw together until they do agree in their conclusions."

President Lowell develops the thought further in connection with the Constitutional Convention of 1787, showing the need which existed to present to the people of the thirteen states a clear-cut alterna-

[9] Baker, *op. cit.,* 1: 137-138.

tive and the impracticability of doing so except by adjustment and perfection in private deliberations of the inchoate and necessarily divergent views which the individual members brought to the sessions of the Convention. Coming then to the specific question of open diplomacy, President Lowell expresses the opinion that, if open diplomacy means that "statesmen of different countries should not be in a position to negotiate a settlement of conflicting views without making public their correspondence and discussions, the plan would defeat its own object. An upright secretary for foreign affairs of each nation must state the whole claims of his own people strongly, and then strive to reach such an agreement as will avoid a conflict or serious friction. It should be his aim so far as possible to prevent ill-feeling between the two peoples over the matter, for ill-feeling of any kind does not tend to amicable relations. If he is obliged to make his statement of claims public, and does not put them strongly, the foreign government will believe that his own countrymen do not take them very seriously and will be less complacent in the matter. If he makes public a strong statement of the claims, he is likely to arouse among a large part of his own people such vigorous sentiments in their favor that it may be hard for him to compromise afterwards. One of the obstacles in rearranging amicably the boundaries of European countries after the war came from the fact that statesmen and writers put forth publicly claims to territory based upon racial, historic, economic, and military grounds, which took such a hold upon the imagination of their peoples that it was well-nigh impossible to reduce them without exciting popular indignation. Many of the claims were wholly irreconcilable with one another, adding greatly to the inherent difficulties of the situation, causing acute friction over the arrangements made, and leaving for the future a legacy of discontent that will not wholly subside for generations yet to come. . . . For good and for evil, but predominantly for good, compromise in human affairs must go on, and compromise does not flourish under the eyes of the multitude."[10]

I quote somewhat at length from President Lowell mainly in order to show that privacy of deliberation is not a peculiar requirement of diplomacy but permeates all government and indeed all human dealings. Its indispensability in diplomacy is a point which need not be labored. In the course of rather an extensive reading of liberal strictures of all sorts upon secret diplomacy I have never found any which did not make some reservation as to the need for a certain amount of secrecy in negotiation.[11] The only real question is the extent of this secrecy, that is, the extent to which the progress of negotiations in particular cases may be, and should be, currently disclosed.

As this question is presented practically from day

[10] *Public opinion in war and peace*, pp. 69 and 154. See also Lord Balfour's statement in the House of Commons, March 19, 1918, *Parl. Debates, Commons*, 5th series, 104: 870 ff.

[11] See for example Borah, William E.: *The perils of secret treaty-making*, in *Forum*, 60: 657 (Dec., 1918); statements by Senator McKellar respecting the meetings of the World War Foreign Debt Commission, *Cong. Rec.*, Jan. 11, 1923, p. 1580; Ponsonby: *Democracy and diplomacy*, pp. 24-26; editorial, *Secret diplomacy*, in *Nation*, 101: 765 (Dec. 30, 1915).

to day in the course of particular negotiations—at an international conference, for example—the answer must be found in the judgment of the plenipotentiaries. There are two opposite points of view between which individual temperament and national tradition vary: (1) a presumption in favor of giving out everything except as there may be specific reasons to the contrary; (2) a presumption against giving out anything except the most formal statements, unless some specific end is to be served. The negative point of view may prevail to a considerable extent, even if it is held by but one of several plenipotentiaries, because unanimity is the rule among the representatives of sovereign states, but it cannot be pushed too far, for, if it is, information will be given out informally and those who deem themselves offended may not care to raise so delicate an issue. On the other hand, publicity at conferences, pushed too far, may defeat itself. When the plenary sessions of the Paris Peace Conference were made open to the public and press correspondents admitted, the effect, we are told, was to make these open sessions largely matters of form.[12] Privacy of initial deliberation will persist in one form or another.

In connection not only with conferences but the everyday proceedings of diplomatic intercourse the present trend is strongly in favor of a maximum of publicity. Aside from any general convictions on the subject which may be held by individual statesmen, there is the insistent need to gain public support. Kennedy, in *Old Diplomacy and New,* relates that in the course of the Fashoda incident (1898) Lord

[12] Baker, *op. cit.,* 1: 150.

Salisbury took the then bold and unusual step of publishing papers during the progress of the negotiations. Within a fortnight of the news of the meeting of the British and French forces at Fashoda and again at the end of the month, all the despatches on the subject were issued to the public, and, Kennedy records, "the public responded to the trust thus reposed in them by a remarkably unanimous support of the Government. Even warlike preparations, such as the formation of a reserve Squadron in the Channel, met with little criticism. Newspapers of Radical opinions approved the strong and direct course which the despatches showed the Government to be pursuing. Prominent Liberal politicians gave their support without stint."

Another frequent motive to publicity is anxiety to forestall the publication of exaggerated and misleading accounts of matters generally known to be afoot. Thus Lord Salisbury in 1890, in reply to a parliamentary inquiry whether it was true that the right of the Germans to fortify Heligoland was to be subject to restrictions, replied: "I think it is a rule that has always been observed in the Foreign Office, and a very valuable rule, that discussions should not take place until negotiations of this kind are concluded. We thought it desirable to issue a despatch for the purpose of stating what our general intentions were; because such matters as these become subjects of discussion and of public comment, and strange and distorted accounts of them are apt to get before the public eye."[13]

Running counter to motives which may dispose

[13] Cited in Heatley: *Diplomacy and the study of international relations*, pp. 263 and 264.

foreign offices to publicity there is the need for protecting sources of information. It is not usually a question of secret information, of which there is very little, but of holding in suitable confidence the candid comments of diplomatic agents abroad. An American Minister was given his passports in 1877 when the Government to which he was accredited discovered among some diplomatic correspondence published in a House report six months before, the following passage from one of the Minister's despatches: "I feel bound to add that there are, in my opinion, only two ways in which the payment of so large an amount can be obtained. The first is by sharing the proceeds with some of the chief officers of this Government; the second, by a display, or, at least, a threat of force. The first course, which has been pursued by one or more nations, will, of course, never be followed by the United States. The expediency of the second it is not my province to discuss."[14]

But much more important than the avoidance of such unfortunate incidents is the imperative necessity of doing nothing in the course of the settlement of particular matters which may hinder compromise and conciliation. To these, as we have seen, untimely publicity may be fatal.

[14] Moore's *Digest*, 4: 535.

CHAPTER VII

THE DISSEMINATION OF INFORMATION

THERE are two kinds of information—general information, or background, and current information. The dissemination of general information is rather the function of publicists and educators than of foreign offices. Foreign offices assist. They publish records of diplomatic correspondence touching matters which have already passed, the volumes appearing sometimes months or years after the events to which they relate. Foreign offices may also make their unpublished archives accessible to scholars down to the latest date believed to be compatible with the public interest.[1] The more particular task of a foreign office under a democracy, however, is the current dissemination of facts touching the actual progress of the country's foreign relations.

Information is disseminated in three principal ways: (1) by official publications, (2) by official utterances, (3) by releases to the press.

1 OFFICIAL PUBLICATIONS

The first officially authorized publication of a treaty in England occurred in 1604. Before that such

[1] Rules are common among European Foreign Ministries establishing dates prior to which students may have unrestricted or limited access to archives. See Barthélemy: *Démocratie et la politique étrangère*, p. 186, for the rules of the French Ministry of Foreign Affairs. The rules of the American State Department are not based upon this rather arbitrary system but leave discretion to a responsible officer of the Department. All possible facilities are given to serious and responsible students.

matters were thought "not fit to be made vulgar." The first officially authorized publication of state papers, including treaties, began a hundred years later. This was Rymer's *Foedera,* comprising twenty volumes published during the period 1704-1732. The original edition was in Latin, but there is an English translation of a later date. A copy of Rymer's *Foedera,* which was used by the Continental Congress, is now in the possession of the Department of State.

All the important governments of the world now publish their treaties soon after ratification. Secret treaties are, of course, not published, but their number is small and probably growing less. In addition to the official series of treaties there are a number of privately compiled treaty collections of great value. Full information respecting them will be found in the article on *Treaties* in the *Encyclopedia Britannica.*

The official publication of treaties occurs in two usual ways: (1) in pamphlet form as part of a numbered treaty series; or (2) in an official gazette. The first procedure obtains in the United States and Great Britain. The American treaty series recently reached No. 668. It is widely distributed and available for public purchase. An American treaty is not published until the President, having received the advice and consent of the Senate, ratifies and proclaims it. Before that it is deemed to be in an inchoate state. The Senate, however, may remove the injunction of secrecy and give out the text. From time to time official compilations are published of all treaties to which the United States has been a party or of treaties in force. The latest compilation consists of two volumes totaling nearly 2,500 pages, published

1910, by authority of the Senate, under the title, *Treaties, Conventions, International Acts, Protocols, and Agreements between the United States of America and other Powers, 1776-1909*, and a third volume, about to come from the press, comprising similar material for the period 1910-1923.[2] The compiler of the first two volumes was Mr. William M. Malloy, clerk of the Senate Committee on Foreign Relations.

The British Government publishes treaties in series form and presents them to Parliament immediately after signature or immediately after the ratification ceremony in case they require to be ratified. The accumulated issues of the series are bound in quinquennial volumes with complete indexes. About once a year a special list is issued of treaty accessions, withdrawals, etc., which have not been considered sufficiently important to publish separately; and particulars of minor engagements and treaty readjustments, which cannot conveniently be included in the treaty series, are printed in the *London Gazette* in the form of Foreign Office notices. Treaty information of special interest to the business community is published in England in the *Board of Trade Journal* and in the United States in *Commerce Reports*, the official publication of the Department of Commerce.

It is the general practice on the continent of Europe to publish treaties in the official gazettes. The same procedure is followed in Japan. Compilations of treaties, conventions, and agreements are also published from time to time.

[2] Senate document, No. 348, 67th Cong., 4th sess. This supersedes a third volume compiled by Mr. Garfield Charles and published by authority of the Senate in 1913.

In addition to treaties, it is now the general custom to publish officially important diplomatic correspondence. The war has familiarized us with books of every conceivable color containing the texts of diplomatic interchanges upon particular subjects. Two principal methods of publication obtain. In the United States and generally in Pan-America an annual conspectus of diplomatic correspondence is issued more or less regularly and more or less promptly. The so-called *Foreign Relations* of the United States have been issued yearly since 1861. They are considered to constitute an appendix to the President's annual message to Congress. The volumes average about 1,000 octavo pages of 500 words each. The bulk of the important diplomatic correspondence of the year is reproduced textually. Professor Denys P. Myers, who has an extraordinarily wide acquaintance with governmental publications, remarks that *Foreign Relations* "is carefully edited and, though not all documents are published, the impression made by it is honest and straightforward." "Omitted from the book," he explains, "are: domestic letters, by which term is understood correspondence originating within the state; large amounts of correspondence relating to claims; a considerable amount of correspondence of an incidental or unimportant relation to the subject handled; and all correspondence with any state which refers to a third state's actions or policy in anything approaching a critical manner."[3]

In Europe the only thing approaching the *Foreign Relations* of the United States is the publication

[3] *The control of foreign relations,* in *Am. Pol. Sci. Rev.,* 11: 45 (Feb., 1917).

known as *British and Foreign State Papers*. This is edited by the Foreign Office and published by the Stationery Office, but is not regarded as a strictly official publication. It contains the texts of British and foreign treaties, legislation, and other documents bearing on international affairs, including selected correspondence from the British parliamentary papers. Volume 113, containing documents for the year 1920, was about to issue from the press early this summer.

The strictly official publications of the British Government, like those of other European countries, are occasional and relate to particular subjects. They are in the form of folio white or blue books and make up ordinarily some two volumes in the annual set of *Parliamentary Papers*. They make no attempt at presenting a conspectus of Foreign Office business during a stated period, but deal extensively with the subjects chosen. Professor Myers says that he has used the modern diplomatic correspondence of most of the Pan-American states, which publish their despatches yearly, and that of Great Britain, France, Portugal, Germany, Austria-Hungary, Italy, and Belgium, which publish correspondence on specific subjects occasionally, and he has found the European publications generally fuller and more satisfactory for the subject dealt with. An exception was Germany which printed not correspondence but a documented argument. The European method, however, in Professor Myers' opinion, leaves much more of the files of Foreign Ministries unprinted. The bulk of the diplomatic correspondence of European chanceries, he says, never sees the light, though the privilege of examination is granted to scholars.

The American system brings out a greater body of correspondence and with greater regularity. Great Britain is the only European state which can be said to publish correspondence regularly, Professor Myers continues, and on the whole the regular publication of correspondence is, in his opinion, the desideratum which should be aimed at.

2 OFFICIAL UTTERANCES

In addition to these publications much official information as to facts and policy transpires through the public utterances of members of the executive addressed to the people or to the legislature. Diplomatic officers at their residences abroad are confined in their public addresses chiefly to the amenities, though public speaking is by tradition a particular duty of our Ambassadors to Great Britain and they have undoubtedly done much to spread common understanding.[4] It is from the members of the Government at home that important statements respecting foreign policy emanate. In general these tend to grow in number and in fullness of discussion, reflecting the increasing need felt for popular support, though of course there is much variation in this respect. By way of concrete illustration, reference may be made to the many public speeches of M. Poincaré on the reparations and Ruhr issues, and

[4] *Cf.* Hendrick: *Life and letters of Walter H. Page,* especially chap. VI, relating to Page's explanations of American policy toward Mexico. See Foster: *The practice of diplomacy,* p. 121, concerning a resolution of censure adopted by the House of Representatives in 1895 anent certain public statements by Bayard, then representing the United States at London. See also Moore's *Digest,* 4: 574.

to President Harding's last address, never actually delivered, which reviewed in a comprehensive and detailed manner the work of his administration in the field of foreign affairs.

Public statements before the legislature are especially important under the parliamentary form of government, where the premier and the minister of foreign affairs are members of one or the other of the chambers and are frequently present at legislative sessions. One recalls Mr. Lloyd George's speeches in the House of Commons before going to the Genoa Conference and upon returning.

Most parliaments receive what amounts to a report on foreign affairs when the foreign office budget is voted. In England this opportunity for discussion seems to have been somewhat neglected recently.[5] In France, as we have already noted, the Budget Committee of the Chamber of Deputies goes thoroughly into the affairs of the Foreign Ministry and its report constitutes a valuable annual record of French policy. At this time, M. Barthélemy relates, "the main lines of diplomatic activity become the subject of a broad academic debate in which several chosen orators of rare talent participate."[6]

Other occasions for giving out information, typical of the parliamentary system, are interpellations and questions. Interpellations in the French Chamber on questions of foreign policy appear to be relatively infrequent, the Government being allowed in practice to choose its own moments to discuss these subjects. Oral questions afford an easier procedure

[5] *Cf.* statement by Mr. Arthur Ponsonby in Commons, March 19, 1918, *Parl. Debates, Commons,* 5th series, 104: 848.

[6] *Démocratie et la politique étrangère,* p. 132.

from a parliamentary point of view, but they also seem to be negligible in number—two in 1907; four in 1908; three in 1909; and one in 1912. A system of written questions was established in 1909, authority being reserved to the Ministry to decline to answer "in the interest of the country." These questions and answers fill columns of the *Bulletin Officiel* and no doubt bring out valuable information, though this seems to be doubted by some.[7] Questions are frequent in British parliamentary practice and elicit much important information.[8]

The imminence of parliamentary inquiry or attack while Parliament is in session keeps the Foreign Office on tiptoe to provide prompt information on all subjects likely to be brought up. Sir E. Hertslet, in his *Recollections of the Old Foreign Office,* relates that in 1850 a member in Parliament made a formal attack in the Commons on Lord Palmerston's foreign policy. The motion was divided into not less than forty headings. To provide material for a complete answer to the charges in this "monster motion," information had to be sought in between 2,000 and 3,000 manuscript volumes. The debate lasted four nights and Palmerston won.

Under the American system the direct contact between the executive and the legislative branches is lacking for the most part. It has been felt by some that the exclusion of the heads of departments from the opportunity to make statements on the floor of

[7] *Cf.* Barthélemy, *op. cit.,* p. 135.

[8] For adverse criticisms of the system of questions, see Young, Geo.: *Diplomacy old and new* (N. Y., 1921), pp. 51 and 52 and statements by Ponsonby in Commons, March 19, 1918, *Parl. Debates, Commons,* 5th series, 104: 848.

Congress was a serious detriment to the public business, and Mr. Hughes has suggested that some means should be found of remedying this situation. Speaking at the University of Michigan in June, 1922, he said:

> Whatever the advantages of our governmental arrangements—and I should be the last to underestimate them—I think it should be candidly admitted that they have the effect of limiting the opportunities for the responsible discussion which aids in the understanding of foreign policy. The conduct of foreign relations pertains to the executive power, and the executive power of the nation is vested in the President, subject to the exceptions and qualifications expressed in the Constitution. Practice under the Constitution has abundantly confirmed the initiative of the President in the formulation of foreign policy.
>
> The wisdom of this disposition of power has been fully demonstrated, for in view of the nature of the task, the delicacy of the negotiations involved, the necessity for promptness, flexibility and unity of control, this authority could not well be lodged elsewhere. But the separateness of the executive power under our system, while it has advantages which have been deemed to be of controlling importance, deprives the executive of the opportunities, open to parliamentary leaders, of participation in parliamentary debates. Official communications are made by the President in the discharge of his constitutional duty. The Department of State, which is the instrumentality of the executive in connection with foreign affairs, makes its public announcements. The Secretary of State appears before committees from time to time and gives the information which is asked. But there is lacking the direct personal relation to the discussions of the Senate when foreign affairs are under consideration. The Secretary of State, acting for the President, may negotiate an important treaty,

but he has no opportunity to explain or defend it upon the floor of the Senate when its provisions are under debate. The knowledge which is at his command is communicated in formal writing or merely to those members who sit upon the appropriate committee. The advantage of oral explication and of meeting each exigency as it arises in the course of discussion and thus of aiding in the formation of public opinion in the manner best adapted to that purpose is not open to him. There are numerous situations in which an opportunity for the executive through his department chiefs to explain matters of policy would be of the greatest aid in securing an intelligent judgment. As President Taft said, "Time and time again debates have arisen in each house upon issues which the information of a particular department head would have enabled him, if present, to end at once by a simple explanation or statement." This is especially true in relation to foreign affairs where the department concerned has sources of information which generally are not available to others.

I should not favor a change in the distribution of power or any modification of practice which would encourage the notion that the executive is responsible to the legislative branch of the government in matters which under the Constitution are exclusively of executive concern. I should also deplore any method so contrived as to facilitate antagonism between the executive department and legislative leaders or which would merely provide opportunities for the censorious. But speaking in my private capacity and expressing only a personal opinion, I do believe in multiplying the facilities for appropriate cooperation between responsible leaders, who understand their respective functions, in a manner suited to the full discussion of great international questions when these fall within the constitutional competency of the Senate. To enable Cabinet officers to vote in either house of Congress would require a constitutional amendment and I should not favor it, but it is quite consistent with our system that the head of a department should have the opportunity personally to be heard where important departmental measures and policies are under consideration. Indeed, the propriety of this method of promoting a better understanding was recognized at the outset, and instead of being foreign to our system it found for a time a place in our original procedure. You will remember that the long continued abstention from such appearances followed the refusal of Congress in 1790 to hear Hamilton when he desired to make in person his Report on the Public Credit. Mischiefs will not be cured by methods which make misapprehension easy. Every facility should be provided, consistent with our system, which will aid in avoiding misconstruction, allaying suspicion and preventing unjust aspersions. The remedy for misunderstanding is explication and debate and the opportunity for thus informing the public judgment in a responsible manner should not be curtailed by any unnecessary artificiality of method.[9]

The President usually devotes a large part of his annual message to foreign affairs, and may transmit special messages in exigent situations. These are formal communications even when delivered personally; there is no debate or interchange of views. Otherwise, and excepting the informal contact of individual members with the executive, information about foreign affairs reaches the American Congress through its committees and by answers to resolutions calling for specific information, if compatible with the public interest. With regard to hearings before committees special reference may be made to the hearings before the Senate Committee on Foreign Relations on the Treaty of Versailles. These fill a volume of 1,300 pages and brought before the

[9] *Am. Jour. Int. Law*, July, 1922, pp. 367-368.

country much important information bearing on a problem of vital importance.[10]

Hearings before legislative committees may or may not be conducted confidentially, but, as secrecy is inverse to the number of participants, the gist of any important information which has been imparted may in any case reach the public. Explanations made by M. Poincaré before the French Foreign Relations Committee March 9, 1923, concerning the situation in the Ruhr were reported in the press in summary form. The appearance of the Premier on this occasion, according to the press report, was to continue a statement begun February 19. It was reported that the Premier had been greatly annoyed by the publicity which had been given to his statements at the earlier meeting. He said that he had been incorrectly reported and canceled a promise he had made to come before the committee a week later. The Committee discovered in due time how the leak had occurred and apologized to him, with the result that he consented again to appear. The press was apparently informed of the gist of what he said on the second occasion.[11]

3 RELEASES TO THE PRESS

The press is the great amplifier. A public speech reaches the ears of only a few. A statement in Parliament is frequently addressed as much to the country at large as to those who hear it. More or less confidential disclosures before parliamentary committees, if important, may soon be noised about. In every case it is the press that actually carries the

[10] Senate document, No. 106, 66th Cong., 1st sess.
[11] Associated Press in Washington *Post,* March 10, 1923.

word to the people. As Bryce remarks, it is the press which has made democracy possible in large countries.

Every foreign ministry maintains direct contact in one way or another with the press. Many have special bureaus for the purpose. One of the most highly developed is the Bureau of Intelligence of the Japanese Foreign Office, which since 1920 has taken on large proportions. Its personnel at a recent date was reported to include 15 officials of the higher civil service, 35 clerks, and 10 or a dozen distinguished journalists and publicists, who are employed as circumstances require to prepare political or economic matter on subjects with which they may be familiar. The importance attached to this bureau is indicated by the fact that the directorship was held until recently by an official of ambassadorial rank. In comparing it with the smaller press bureaus of some other foreign ministries it is necessary, however, to bear in mind that the Japanese bureau attends to the dissemination not only of general and political information but also economic reports from Japanese representatives abroad, a function which, in the United States, for example, was taken over by another department twenty years ago and has since been developed on a large scale.

Foreign ministries have three methods of giving information to the press which they may employ separately or concurrently—(1) formal written *communiqués,* (2) oral conferences with a body of the press representatives, or (3) individual interviews. Of the first there is, of course, an infinite variety, both as to character and frequency. At the bottom of the gamut is the policy of making communications only when it is deemed necessary to correct erroneous and harmful reports. The written *communiqués* given out at the American State Department vary in frequency with the progress of events, but over a considerable period average probably one or two a day.

At a number of foreign ministries there are daily conferences between a high official and the press representatives in a body. Speaking of "the paramount importance of contact with the press," Secretary Hughes recently described the extent to which this system has been carried in the United States. "Occasionally public announcements are expected," he explained, "but the representatives of the press desire to write in their own way and to obtain material by their own inquiries. What is desired is not control of news but accurate information. To meet this demand, the President himself meets the correspondents twice a week and Department Heads still more frequently. The Secretary of State has two press conferences each working day at which either the Secretary or the Under Secretary is present. The officers are not quoted, but there is frank disclosure of facts and aims within the widest possible limits. There is thus the most direct contact with those who are the principal purveyors of information and the chief educators of the public."[12]

Daily press conferences are not the rule at the British Foreign Office, but they are called from time to time. On occasion very frank statements are given out in writing. When Lord Curzon returned from the first session of the Lausanne Conference, he gave

[12] Address at the University of Michigan, June, 1922.

to the press a defense of his course there which went into considerable detail. It was nearly 2,000 words in length and wound up as follows:

> Of course I know that in some quarters I shall be taunted with failure or held accountable for a breakdown, where I have been battling not for myself, not even for British interests alone, but for allied unity and the cause of genuine peace, and where the responsibility rested with the Turkish delegation, and them alone. . . . I am content to be judged by the results.[13]

The British as well as other delegations at recent international conferences have maintained close relations with the press representatives. Lord Riddell, himself a journalist, met them daily at both Paris and Washington and gave an informal summary of the proceedings from the British point of view. Relations with the press at international conferences have become something of a game. At almost every conference there is complaint that one or more delegations are endeavoring to color the news for their own purposes. Rumors may be started by unofficial persons or by particular interests. At the Lausanne Conference the American representatives found it necessary to issue a public statement denying repeated rumors that they had suggested a postponement or adjournment of the conference, and adding that when the occasion was presented the

[13] New York *Times*, Feb. 7, 1923. See *Times* of October 17, 1922, for a very frank statement to the press made by M. Franklin Bouillon upon returning to Paris from the Mudania Conference. It was the pacific policy of France, he is reported to have said, combined with the sincere desire of Mustapha Kemal to avoid war and not the British display of force which prevented war in the Near East.

American delegation would not hesitate to expose the original source of such misrepresentation.[14]

Mr. Lloyd George's close relations with the press are a well-known feature of his manner of conducting foreign relations. We are indebted to a serious British journalist, who suggests that he may have carried the system too far, for the following interesting and illuminating incident:

On the occasion of one of the post-war Conferences in Paris, the author, together with other British and American journalists, was invited to a dinner party by Lord Riddell, at which it was announced the Prime Minister would be present. Mr. Lloyd-George duly appeared, rather late, having refreshed himself elsewhere, for the express purpose, we were informed, of answering any questions which we liked to address to him. The Conference was not ended; so negotiations with the French Government were still proceeding. The knowledge of this fact did not prevent some of the American journalists present from asking leading questions. "Mr. Prime Minister," queried one, "are you on good terms with M. Briand?" (then French Prime Minister). Other enquiries, more insinuating and more indiscreet, were freely put, and ambiguously assented to, or cleverly evaded, by Mr. Lloyd-George. The performance resolved itself into a duel of wits, in which the questioners thrust and the questioned parried. Some of the answers certainly illuminated or explained; others, when the information demanded was on a delicate subject, obtained, and could only obtain, an insincere or misleading reply. A meeting between negotiators and journalists is certainly much appreciated by the latter, and may perhaps be of mutual advantage. But it should be of a frankly social nature, wherein acquaintance may be made, the personal element gauged, and mutual confidence established. For

[14] New York *Tribune,* Dec. 3, 1922.

the Minister to pretend to answer questions which cannot properly be answered at the time, is to promote insincerity and prevarication, and to revive the odium into which diplomacy had fallen with the public, and which its democratization is calculated to dispel.[15]

Journalists of good standing can usually obtain individual interviews with foreign office officials upon request and within the practical limits imposed by the pressure of foreign office work. Such interviews are naturally more frequent where there are not daily conferences with the whole body of press representatives. Foreign office officials may occasionally send for particular journalists and discuss with them pending matters with a view to assuring an accurate statement of the facts or possibly a strong presentation of one aspect of a situation. It is known that certain newspapers are especially close to their respective ministries. The London *Times* used to occupy a special position at the British Foreign Office.[16] Statements in the Paris *Temps* concerning French foreign policy are usually taken to have a well-grounded significance. Some of the telegraph agencies and press associations present the official point of view. This is useful to the public, if it is understood, and frequently serves the cause of international understanding. It may also on occasion serve the ends of official propaganda.

It is hardly necessary to enter at length upon

[15] Kennedy: *Old diplomacy and new,* pp. 287 and 288. See New York *Times* for Sept. 24, 1922, for a vivid account of one of Mr. Lloyd George's press conferences in Downing Street.

[16] *Cf.* Johnston, Sir Harry: *Common sense in foreign policy* (London, 1913), p. 2, and Cook, Sir Edward: *Delane of the Times* (London, 1916), espe. chap. X.

THE DISSEMINATION OF INFORMATION 127

propaganda in its relation to foreign affairs. It is a subject which has been pretty well aired. "Propaganda," says Bertrand Russell, "conducted by the means which advertisers have found successful, is now one of the recognized methods of government in all advanced countries, and is especially the method by which democratic opinion is created."[17] It is new only in its extent and the intensity of its method. At the Congress of Westphalia in 1648 "Pamphleteering abounded" and "there were frequent appeals to the public opinion of Europe."[18] It was a serious business with the American Government in its early days[19] and during the Civil War,[20] as well as on the occasion of the late world struggle. We are disposed to regard propaganda of this kind as justified and necessary, and within certain limits altogether admirable. Of quite a different character are the methods for which Bismarck showed the way and

[17] *Free thought and official propaganda* (N. Y., 1922), p. 38. For an interesting discussion of the Ministry of Information which was set up in England during the war, see *Parl. Debates, Commons,* 5th series, 109: 947-1035, Aug. 5, 1918.

[18] Bernard, Mountague: *Lectures on diplomacy* (London, 1868), pp. 24 and 25.

[19] "It is necessary for America to have agents in different parts of Europe, to give some information concerning our affairs, and to refute the abominable lies that the hired emissaries of Great Britain circulate in every corner of Europe, by which they keep up their own credit and ruin ours. I have been more convinced of this since my peregrinations in this country than ever. The universal and profound ignorance of America here has astonished me. It will require time and a great deal of prudence and delicacy to undeceive them." J. Adams to Franklin, Oct. 14, 1780, 7 *John Adams' works,* 317, cited in Moore's *Digest,* 4: 431 and 432.

[20] See Foster: *Century of American diplomacy,* p. 398; Moore's *Digest,* 4: 446-447.

the official subventions to newspapers which are said to be common on the continent.[21] But such abuses tend to correct themselves. It is well known that directed to selfish ends propaganda soon provokes a reaction. At the Paris Peace Conference it was carried to absurd limits; and the public, as well as public men, have become correspondingly wary.

An interesting latter-day development has been lecturers of a semi-official character. Those from England, who have rather bombarded us since the war, have had for the most part a courteous and attentive hearing. Lord Robert Cecil's advocacy of the League was well received and no doubt furnished good food for public thought, in whatever direction its influence may have lain. M. Clemenceau's visit was also accepted in the spirit in which it was conceived. Members of the American Senate among others welcomed the opportunity for discussion of a great public issue.[22]

[21] *Cf.* Barthélemy, *op. cit.*, p. 187.
[22] See *Cong. Rec.*, Nov. 23, 1922, pp. 49 and 53.

CHAPTER VIII

PUBLIC OPINION ON FOREIGN AFFAIRS

How public opinion is formed in general is a matter beyond the scope of our inquiry. There are some interesting and instructive books on the subject,[1] though hardly as many as one might expect. For our purpose it is only necessary to refer to some of the difficulties connected with the formation of public opinion on foreign affairs.

In order to maintain a sound public opinion, three things are essential. The public must have a more or less sustained interest, it must be informed, and its conclusions must be reached mainly by rational processes. It is at once apparent that these conditions are least assured in the realm of foreign affairs. The interest of the public is for the most part weak and intermittent, information is relatively difficult to obtain and is least dependable, and there is a strong play of sentiment.

Public interest responds naturally to matters which affect closely the daily lives of the members of the community, and less certainly to matters which touch the imagination.[2] It is self-evident, therefore, as a general proposition, that foreign, as contrasted with domestic, affairs have an uncertain appeal to the general attention. If this needs demonstration, the proof is found in the exceptions.

---

[1] *E.g.*, Lowell: *Public opinion and popular government* (New York, 1921), and *Public opinion in war and peace* (Cambridge, 1923); Lippmann, Walter: *Public opinion* (New York, 1922). See also Bryce: *Modern democracies,* chap. xv.

[2] *Cf.* Lowell: *Public opinion and popular government,* p. 53.

There are miscellaneous persons of education who maintain a somewhat constant interest in foreign affairs because it is to their taste and responds to feelings of patriotic pride and interest, but their number in any country is relatively very small. The interests of the mercantile and financial classes, especially of the seaboard regions, are often directly influenced by conditions abroad and the relation of their country to them, and their attention to the foreign field may therefore be fairly well sustained. The regular employment of large bodies of factory workers in England is directly connected with the state of foreign markets, and they evince an interest correspondingly keen in matters which are likely to affect the volume of orders from particular foreign regions. A large element in the population of the United States, the western farmer and rural townsman whom Bryce selected as the characteristic type of our "average citizen,"[3] have not until recently—since the opening of the Mississippi River to navigation in 1803—been perceptibly affected in their personal interests by foreign affairs, but the reflex of the situation in Europe on the market for farm products has turned their attention in that direction, and a number of their representatives in Congress have thought it worth while to cross the Atlantic to study conditions at first-hand, whereas only a short time ago such trips would hardly have been thought of.

It is undoubtedly true that the change from national to world economy is arousing a more general interest in international relations. Sir Edward Grigg

[3] *Modern democracies*, 2: 119.

told us the other evening of the lively concern of his Manchester constituents in the progress of the situation in the Near East. Another stimulant to popular interest is the general acceptance of the principle of compulsory military service. The possibility of war now suggests realities to nearly every member of the body politic. Yet interest easily lags. It is necessary to remember that we are in the midst of special conditions. We have just gone through the worst war in history, and there is none who has not been directly touched by it. The world is still in tumult, and everyone is alive to the possibility of further conflict and its calamitous results. Just now, therefore, the public interest in foreign affairs is relatively strong and well sustained, but this condition cannot be counted upon to continue. On the contrary, it is the devout hope of all that the world will soon mend. Then each nation can settle back into a comfortable preoccupation with its own affairs. "For a long time," wrote a member of the French Chamber in an official report in 1903, "we have observed the sort of indifference with which the French parliament looks upon questions of foreign policy and abandons that regular and minute control without which ministerial responsibility is only a fiction. In this attitude it but reflects too accurately the state of mind of a country to which cruel and too numerous lessons have not been sufficient to teach the capital interest of these problems and their reaction upon the prosperity and even the security of the nation."[4]

Foreign affairs have a special appeal to the imagination undoubtedly. Among the broader masses of a

[4] Cited in Barthélemy: *Démocratie et la politique étrangère,* p. 126.

democracy, however, the imagination is stirred only by occasional and spectacular events and cannot be counted upon to contribute to a sustained public opinion. It must be confirmed that in general foreign affairs occupy a decidedly secondary place in the public mind. They come to the fore only after acute situations have developed or some great issue has been joined. To the vast majority of problems that arise daily in the intercourse of states the body of the public remains indifferent.

It is equally self-evident as a general proposition that the public is less well informed about foreign than about domestic matters. The element of direct observation is almost altogether lacking. Foreign affairs lie in the "unseen environment," and knowledge of them must come through media which are operating under the same disadvantages of distance.

The principal channel for current information is the press. It is difficult to speak in measured terms of what the press is doing. Its system of gathering information the world over and relating events almost as they happen is one of the monumental achievements of the age. We must note, however, deficiencies in respect to foreign affairs which are not for the most part the fault of the press but exist in the nature of things.

Though there is a highly developed sense of public duty in the newspaper profession, the publishing of newspapers remains a commercial enterprise. Readers are needed to build up advertising patronage, and readers are obtained by interesting the public. The comparatively minor and sporadic interest of the public in foreign affairs is therefore reflected in the subject matter of newspaper columns. A classification made in 1900 of the subject matter of more than 9,000 columns in 110 newspapers published in fourteen large cities of the United States showed, on the average, after deducting advertising matter, 81 per cent of the space devoted to news, 5 per cent to illustrations, 3.5 per cent to literature, and 10.5 per cent to opinion (editorials and letters). The 81 per cent of news was made up of 26 per cent war news, 32 per cent general news, and 23 per cent special news (business, sporting, society). The 32 per cent of general news comprised 1.8 per cent foreign, 9.4 political, 4.6 crime, and 16.3 miscellaneous.[5] This represented the averaged estimate, probably pretty accurate, of the editors of those 110 newspapers of the distribution of the interest of their reading public.

Since 1900 the press of most countries, except possibly that of England, which has long emphasized this department, has come to print more foreign news. A well-known French journalist recalls that when he entered journalism twenty years ago "the room devoted to the foreign news in most of the papers was very small indeed: some lines, perhaps half a column, for many of them, and no more."[6] Now frequently there are many columns in the big metropolitan dailies. The foreign news services of a number of well-known papers in the United States have been admirably developed in recent years. Long and detailed accounts of the progress of affairs in Europe are provided and sometimes the full text, trans-

[5] Lippmann: *Public opinion*, p. 62.
[6] Recouly, Raymond: *Journalism and international politics*, in *Harper's Magazine*, Dec., 1922. See also on this subject, Given, John L.: *Making a newspaper* (New York, 1907), chap. xiii.

mitted by cable, of important state papers. This is most helpful to the formation of sound opinion, especially among those who give particular attention to foreign affairs and editors and other secondary centres of distribution. It must be kept in mind, nevertheless, that the readers of the few papers that do this sort of thing, especially in a big country like the United States, do not represent the whole public or even a large part of it. It was authoritatively stated some years ago that of 2,300 dailies published in the United States only about 175 were printed in cities of more than 100,000 population. These 175 are the papers which compose the great press associations and get the news from abroad, and it is through them that the foreign news in abbreviated form reaches the smaller press.[7] It is this smaller press which constitutes the direct news source of the bulk of the people, and the room which it gives to the foreign despatches, even in the case of papers fairly remote from metropolitan competition, is ordinarily very small indeed.

The determining factor is the interest of the public, and such evidence as is at hand does not indicate that there has been, since 1900, such an increase in the general interest in foreign affairs as one might expect who did not take into account the constant devotion of people to the matters which immediately surround them. Replies obtained in 1916 from 2,300 prominent business and professional men in Chicago —a picked public—indicated that among about 70 per cent who based their newspaper preference on the treatment of public affairs 18 per cent were

[7] Lippmann, *op. cit.*, p. 324; Given, *op. cit.*, pp. 13 and 222.

primarily interested in local news, 16 per cent in political, 11 per cent in financial, 9.5 per cent in foreign, 7 per cent in general news, and 9 per cent in editorials. A questionnaire sent in 1920 to 1,761 men and women college students in New York City, asking what "five features" interested them the most in newspapers, elicited from the portion (67 per cent) interested in public affairs generally a 20 per cent preference for "general news," 15 per cent for editorials, 12 per cent for "politics," 8 per cent for finance, only a little over 6 per cent for foreign news, 3½ per cent for local news, and about 3 per cent for business news.[8]

It is interesting to note also that the bulk of the persons addressed in these inquiries said that they devoted to the newspapers "about fifteen minutes a day," or say not more than half an hour. The replies from the 2,300 prominent business and professional men of Chicago indicated that 14 per cent read but one newspaper, 46 per cent two, 21 per cent three, 10 per cent four, and 8 per cent more than four.

"No elaborate deductions are to be drawn from these figures," writes Mr. Walter Lippmann. "They help merely to make somewhat more concrete our notions of the effort that goes day by day into acquiring the data of our opinions. The newspapers are, of course, not the only means, but they are certainly the principal ones. Magazines, the public forum, the Chautauqua, the church, political gatherings, trade union meetings, women's clubs, and news serials in the moving picture houses supplement the press. But

[8] Lippmann, *op. cit.*, p. 60.

taking it all at the most favorable estimate, the time each day is small when any of us is directly exposed to information from our unseen environment.'"[9] Mr. Lippmann is speaking of public affairs generally. The restrictions apply *a fortiori* to foreign affairs.

In a good many instances the foreign news is reported accurately and intelligently. Some of the special correspondents have attained distinction as acute and impartial observers. The intelligence of the reporter remains nevertheless a factor. The French journalist quoted above speaks especially of the difficulty of finding clever and well-educated men who really know the subjects upon which they are expected to write. Mr. Ray Stannard Baker, a newspaper man himself, reverts frequently in his account of the Peace Conference to the want of background among many of the American correspondents who flocked to Paris, some of whom had never before been out of the United States and had no acquaintance with the conditions, problems, personalities, history, and tradition which lay back of that great drama.[10]

The incomplete and frequently intermittent character of the press records must also be taken into account. Referring to the historical records of diplomatic negotiations which usually become available in due time, Professor Myers remarks that "if one will compare such a complete record with contemporary press accounts, he will clearly realize how much out of perspective the latter are; not from dishonesty but simply from the incompleteness of the

[9] Lippmann, *op. cit.*, p. 63.
[10] *Woodrow Wilson and the world settlement,* chaps. vii and viii.

record.''[11] The intermittent character of the press reports of foreign affairs was emphasized by Mr. Arthur Ponsonby in parliamentary debate in 1918. "What happens in the press?" he said. "We see a series of events reported with great fullness; we begin to read of them. The next day the story continues, and we read it with interest; but the day after that some domestic concern crops up, either in parliament or in the country, and the foreign news is withdrawn, the story stops, the country is under the impression that that particular issue is over. It may not be at all.''[12]

Another difficulty is sensationalism. Among the better papers the most frequent manifestation of this fault is untrue emphasis in the writing of headlines—those summaries which constitute the whole reading of many persons, especially with respect to foreign affairs. In the yellow press it often takes a form which cannot be too strongly regretted and condemned—the abuse of friendly but foreign peoples. The yellow editors and cartoonists apparently do not hesitate at the grossest misrepresentations. The disposition to belittle what is foreign is, I suppose, an aspect of nationalism. It crops out in milder form even in the more serious press. "Speaking broadly," writes Bryce, "it must be confessed that the press of all the nations taken together has done much to set them in an unlovely light to one another and said more to provoke enmity than to win friendship.''[13] The unfair presentation of international

[11] *The control of foreign relations*, in *Am. Pol. Sci. Rev.*, 11: 44.
[12] *Parl. Debates, Commons*, 5th series, 104: 854, March 19, 1918.
[13] *International relations*, p. 143. "It is small wonder," writes Mr. Walter Lippmann, "that newspapers are in the main instru-

controversies is another phase of the same thing. "Before the outbreak of the war between the United States and Spain in 1898," writes Bryce in another place, "the newspapers of the former country were deluged with matter putting the conduct of Spain in Cuba—conduct doubtless open to grave censure—in the worst light and letting little or nothing appear on her behalf. A more remarkable case was seen a year later, when the bulk of the British press stated and exaggerated what case there was against the Transvaal Government, while ignoring the facts which made in favour of that republic, with the result that the British public never had the data necessary for forming a fair judgment."[14]

Quite as important as sources of current information is the possession by the citizen of a fund of general knowledge against which to apply the daily reports. The special handicaps existing in the realm of foreign affairs are again apparent. It is difficult to visualize situations against a new background. The picture is projected naturally in the light of one's own surroundings. Factors such as popular mentality and education, standards of living, the means of communication and transport, are unconsciously included in their familiar forms, though

---

ments of irritation between peoples. I leave out of account here the deliberately pacificist press as well as the reptile press of the war parties. It is the ordinary middle-class newspapers which I have in mind, the papers run as commercial enterprises. With all their faults admitted, no one can possibly assert that their owners are criminal enough to provoke war. Yet in almost every crisis the tension is increased by the newspapers." (*The stakes of diplomacy*, p. 54.)

[14] *Modern democracies*, 1: 100.

they may be in fact entirely different in the situation which is in question.

"The masses of the people," writes Bryce, "do not in any European country know enough of foreign countries to enable them to form sound opinions in particular crises."[15] In the United States, as a natural result of our position and history, even the better informed are frequently deficient in any general knowledge of other peoples. Speaking of this in the House of Representatives last February Mr. Meyer London ventured the opinion that "the educated American knows more about ancient Rome and Greece than about France, Austria, Germany, or any of the continental countries of Europe."[16]

It is interesting to note in this connection the results of a recent survey of 510 catalogues of American colleges and professional schools. The purpose was to ascertain the extent to which subjects directly related to foreign affairs were taught. Of the 510 catalogues examined, 325 were found not to mention such subjects at all. Of the remaining 185 which dealt little or much with foreign affairs, seven announced courses in present-day world policies; 40 in contemporary history, starting usually about 1870; 25 in comparative governments, largely remote and historical; and 10 in the World War and its results. Of 14 colleges for women with 11,000 students, none, according to this investigation, announced a course on the World War; one gave a special course in current events; and seven stated that current topics were used in connection with other periods.[17]

[15] *International relations*, p. 186.
[16] *Cong. Rec.*, March 5, 1923, p. 5554.
[17] Barnes, Julius: *Foreign affairs; a neglected study*, in New York *Times*, Jan. 21, 1923.

On the other hand, it is undoubtedly the case in this country, and presumably to varying degrees in others, that the general public knowledge of foreign affairs and appreciation of foreign conditions are growing. The American institutions of learning which do teach subjects directly related to foreign affairs are probably the larger ones which reach the greater number of students, and the number of such courses tends to increase. Of 600 colleges and universities listed with the United States Bureau of Education in 1922 about one-tenth reported courses in training for foreign trade and foreign service of the Government.[18] The teaching of history and foreign literature progresses. The history textbooks of the lower schools are said to have been improved.

The public is gaining background in other ways. Foreign travel becomes more general and far-reaching. The development of photography must be noted. The educative effect of the World War was incalculable for those who remained at home as well as those who went abroad. The increase in foreign subjects in books and periodicals in the last few years has been marked, and I am told that a strikingly large proportion of doctoral theses and academic studies now relate to international affairs. At least four new magazines dealing wholly or in part with foreign affairs have been started in this country within the past year. There is a wider discussion of foreign affairs in clubs and societies. The activity of the League of Women Voters in promoting in many cities round-table discussions of subjects in this field may be noted.

[18] Bureau of Education, Commercial Education Circular No. 11, Jan. 15, 1923.

While progress in this general direction is encouraging, it is always necessary to recall that we are in the midst of a special period, when foreign affairs are brought much to the fore by conditions which we should like to see abated in large part; and President Lowell, writing with respect to public affairs in general, makes the discouraging suggestion that the spread of information and understanding through the mechanical development of the means of travel and communication may not after all be keeping pace with the growing complexity of the affairs which have to be understood.[19]

We have finally to note the part which sentiment plays in international questions. An experienced American journalist wrote a few years ago that American public opinion on international affairs rests upon sentiment alone.[20] Certainly sentiment is an important element in human judgment generally. Its influence is sometimes good,[21] but in the field of foreign affairs it produces too often that unreasoning intolerance which is one of the unfortunate concomitants of nationalism. It is unnecessary to expatiate on the obstacles created thereby to the formation of a reasonable view of international problems. The evil effects are not limited to the racially crowded confines of Europe. We see them reproduced on our own soil by the sentimental attachments and traditions of immigrant groups.

When we set the intricacies of international problems over against these special obstacles to the

[19] Lowell, *op. cit.*, p. 48.
[20] Carey, Edward: *Journalism and international affairs*, in *International Conciliation*, Aug., 1909, No. 21.
[21] *Cf.* Lowell, *op. cit.*, p. 16.

formation of a sound, sustained public opinion, the difficulties of the situation become at once apparent. In almost all international problems there are "complicated states of fact which cannot be understood without an intimate knowledge of historical background and a painstaking and discriminating analysis of material. There are situations of controlling importance that are wholly unknown to the general public, and which cannot be appreciated without the special information available only to officers of the Government."[22] The fact is that on the great bulk of international problems, especially in their initial stages, there can be no public opinion at all. But there emerge from these problems from time to time broad and comparatively simple issues which the people must decide and with respect to which, it has been found,[23] their fundamental common sense asserts itself as it has proved to do with respect to their domestic concerns. Those who are charged with the conduct of the foreign relations of a democracy are deprived in large part of the current guidance of public opinion. They must proceed with their daily work in accordance with their best judgment and in the light of tradition and precedent, taking care to direct public attention to important matters as they develop and to supply the data about which public opinion may crystallize.

[22] Hughes: *Some observations on the conduct of our foreign relations*, in *Am. Jour. Int. Law*, 16: 366.

[23] *Cf.* Bryce: *Modern democracies*, chap. lxi, *Democracy and foreign policy;* also *International relations*, pp. 186 and 187.

CHAPTER IX

CRYSTALLIZATION AND ENFORCEMENT OF OPINION THROUGH THE LEGISLATURE

THE crystallization and the enforcement of opinion are to a great extent inseparable processes. Opinion crystallizes in the process of enforcement and enforces itself in the process of crystallization. As an incident to the enforcement of opinion there is frequently debate or deliberation, which has a tendency to alter the view sought to be enforced. On the other hand, each expression of opinion in an important quarter has its particular effect. Each forum of debate has means, more or less effective, whereby its judgments may make themselves felt.

The first instrumentality for the crystallization and enforcement of opinion with regard to foreign affairs is the national legislature.

The pursuit of foreign policy, as we have seen, rests primarily in the hands of the executive. Legislatures have not been able to assert in this field the detailed control which they have acquired over domestic affairs. This is made clear by Bryce in Chapter XXI of *The American Commonwealth*. The legislative branch, he observes, tends always to encroach upon the executive. Its principal means to this end, in large modern states, is to frame its laws with such particularity as to provide by anticipation for the greatest possible number of imaginable cases and in this way so to bind down its officials as to leave them no volition, no real authority. Wherever the will of the people prevails, Bryce points out, the legislature may, since it represents the people, make itself omnipotent by this means, unless it is checked by the action of the people themselves. This is so with respect to domestic affairs. But, he continues, foreign affairs, in sharp distinction therefrom, cannot be provided for beforehand in this way by laws general in application but minutely particular in wording. Discretion must perforce be left to the executive, more especially as the foreign relations of modern states have become so numerous and complex that a large popular assembly can have neither the time nor requisite knowledge for handling even the ordinary business, much less to conduct delicate negotiations requiring promptitude and discretion. The result is that, while in the domestic field alone the legislative branch tends to extinguish the executive as a power in the state, the importance of foreign policy and the practical difficulty of taking it out of the hands of the executive are so great that the executive easily maintains its leadership in this department and may even draw therefrom an influence reacting in favor of its weight and dignity in the whole field of government.

In parliamentary governments the executive is recruited from the legislature. There may then be, as in England,[1] a tendency on the part of the legislature to relax somewhat the stringency of its statutory control. But the distinction between the legislature and the executive is not obliterated. The executive for the time being represents normally but one party or group of parties, while the whole legislature, in

[1] *Cf.* Bryce: *American commonwealth,* 1: 219.

theory at any rate, is a reduced facsimile of the thought and sentiment of the nation. What is more important is the existence of a legislative state of mind and an executive state of mind. These may be, and usually are, taken on by the same individual as he passes from one branch to the other. The legislative mind, relieved from the pressure of administrative and executive responsibilities, and in direct touch with the constituencies, is more sensitive to the currents of public thought and feeling, and is by nature disposed to criticism. The executive mind, on the other hand, is more directly exposed to the pressure of actual situations and seeks to dispose of problems promptly and advantageously but with the least to-do consistent with the public interest. In parliamentary governments, except among the extremists, who cannot hope to succeed to power, the critical disposition of the legislator is tempered by the restraining thought that tomorrow the critic may be called upon to perform. Under the presidential form of government the legislator is further removed from that potential embarrassment, but the sincerity and sense of fair play of individual members and party responsibility operate in the same direction.

The disposition of legislative bodies to concern themselves with foreign politics has not been favored by the later developments of democracy. The alteration in the character and interests of the individual members and the great pressure of domestic affairs resulting from the advance in material civilization and the extension of governmental initiative and control into many departments of economic and social endeavor, have combined to crowd foreign affairs from the legislative calendars. This has been especially noticed in the British Parliament. Referring to the subject in a debate on the control of foreign relations in 1918—and it would certainly be even more true today—Mr. Arthur Ponsonby remarked upon the change which had come over the membership of the House of Commons in the past ten years. The advent of men of moderate means and a large number of Labor members had brought into the House many who had a very special knowledge of the domestic problems which had been so much before Parliament recently. At the same time there had been a reduction in the number of members who had any close knowledge of foreign affairs. The result had been to give the country a false impression that foreign affairs were not on the same level of importance with domestic affairs.[2]

Much the same view was expressed by another English Liberal, Mr. G. Lowes Dickinson, writing in 1916, when he said: "In England, and no doubt in other countries, it is plainly true that the advent of democracy has meant, so far, not more but less interest in foreign policy. The new classes admitted to the franchise have, naturally enough, concentrated their interest on the domestic legislation that bears directly on the conditions of their life. This legislation, more and more, has taken up the time and attention of Parliament."[3]

Statistics show indeed that in the period 1801-1810 foreign relations occupied about 27 per cent of the Commons debates, whereas in the period 1881-1890

[2] *Parl. Debates, Commons*, 5th series, 104: 852.
[3] *Democratic control of foreign policy*, in *Atlantic Monthly*, August, 1916, p. 149.

they occupied but 12 per cent,[4] a difference which cannot be accounted for altogether by the Napoleonic wars.

The situation in the British Parliament is somewhat special.[5] However, the tendency of the modern legislator to become absorbed in home affairs exclusively may be observed in the United States also, in connection, for example, with the so-called radical bloc in Congress. When this was first organized in December, 1922, there was discussion in the press of the points of foreign policy for which it would stand, speculation including, for instance, recognition of the Soviet régime in Russia. Yet so far there has been a complete absence of foreign issues from the programme which this group has actually pursued. The United States came recently to a fork in the highway of foreign relations, and the need to choose a way has militated against the natural preoccupation of the legislative branch with internal problems. Still foreign affairs have not had a large place in the debates of the House. If it has been different in the Senate,

[4] Spalding: *Federation and empire*, p. 79.
[5] Lord Balfour has expressed the view that the comparative neglect of foreign affairs in the British Parliament during recent years has been due more than anything else to the absence of sharp party differences with respect to these affairs (Ponsonby: *Democracy and diplomacy*, pp. 121-127). Speaking before the House in 1911 Lord Grey said: "The real reason for lack of control . . . is the congestion of business in the House of Commons. . . . As long as the House of Commons remains without some great measure of devolution, its business will be so congested that, with the best will in the world, they would never be able to acquire that control of imperial policy which it can only acquire by frequent debates on important subjects." (*Parl. Debates, Commons*, 5th series, 24: 540.)

the reason is no doubt to be found in the special duties imposed upon that body by the Constitution.

If the position of the legislative branch in the field of foreign affairs is not so completely dominant as in the domestic field and if there is a disposition on the part of legislatures to neglect those affairs in favor of domestic problems, still the legislature remains the paramount instrumentality for crystallizing opinion with respect to foreign policy and particularly for enforcing it. Its authority, when it cares to exercise it, is decisive. Let us examine briefly the practical working of some of the principal democratic legislatures as forums of debate and as corporate instruments for guiding, and if need be controlling, the executive pursuit of foreign policy, first, with respect to treaties, then with respect to foreign policy outside of the realm of treaties, and finally with respect to the question of peace or war.

The Senate of the United States appears preeminent among legislative bodies as a medium for the crystallization and enforcement of opinion with respect to treaties. It may be observed in general that, the initiative being with the executive, the interest of legislatures in foreign affairs is neither continuous nor logical in its emphasis. It is aroused by concrete events as they occur and responds to the measure of public, and partisan, interest. Now the submission to the Senate of an important treaty is a conspicuous event. The same process occurs in other democratic countries, but in many of them political treaties, which have a vital interest for the people, do not have to be submitted; and, when treaties are submitted, approval is facilitated by the working of parliamentary government, unless a ministerial crisis be precipitated. In the case of the United States Senate the sheer difficulty of obtaining the acquiescence of two-thirds of a quorum not only leads to thoroughgoing examination and debate in the Senate itself, but assures also the keenest public interest. Whatever of partisanship, or of personal feeling, may have entered into the contest over the Treaty of Versailles—and whatever individual judgment of the outcome may be—the fact remains that the debate in the Senate, conducted in open session, served most effectively the purpose of arousing popular interest, placing information before the country, and forming opinion.

By contrast the procedure of the French Chambers, when treaties are submitted for approval, is more attuned to the intricacies and amenities of world politics and is less effective in arousing and crystallizing the thought and feeling of the nation. At Paris the emphasis is strongly on the work of the committees. A committee's examination of a proposed treaty is often long and thorough. The debate before the Chamber, just as frequently, is brief and superficial. "Thus"—recounts Barthélemy—"the treaty of March 15, 1874, which established our protectorate over Annam and contained the germ of our colonial expansion, retained for scarcely an hour the attention of the National Assembly. It was voted without discussion, almost without comment (July 7, 1875). The Treaty of Berlin of February 26, 1885, which laid down the most important principles of public law affecting Africa, was approved August 3, 1885, by 251 votes against 96 after an insignificant discussion.'"[6] The procedure has not been different in the case of the Washington Conference treaties.

The French Chambers have, moreover, less effective means of enforcing their views in respect to treaties. In the first place, as we have seen, legislative approval is required only for certain descriptions of treaties. Then with respect to these the Chambers have but the alternative of yes or no.[7] The American expedient of "reservations" is not employed, though there has been talk of it in connection with the Washington treaties, and on occasion an *ordre de jour* may be voted directing the executive to undertake further negotiations.[8] The French Chambers must under these circumstances have consented sometimes to ratification only because it appeared less desirable to throw over entirely the work of the executive than to accept a result not altogether satisfactory. The American Senate also has probably been influenced at times by this way of thinking, but it early took to itself, and has frequently used, the right of interpreting or amending, while approving as interpreted or amended, treaties signed by the executive. These reservations are subject to the willingness of the executive to proceed with them and of the foreign government to accept them, but, as Mathews has pointed out,[9] when they are accepted, the Senate as a body has in effect participated directly in the

[6] *Démocratie et la politique étrangère,* pp. 131 and 132.

[7] Michon: *Les traités internationaux devant les chambres,* p. 204; Chow: *Le contrôle parlementaire de la politique étrangère,* p. 170.

[8] *Cf.* Stuart: *French foreign policy,* p. 131.

[9] *The conduct of American foreign relations,* pp. 155-156.

negotiation of the treaty. Of approximately 650 signed treaties the United States Senate has refused consent to ratification in the case of about 20 and has qualified its consent in the case of about 70.[10]

The American constitutional requirement that all treaties should have legislative sanction has commended itself to many of those in Europe who seek in their own countries further to democratize methods of conducting foreign affairs, but, realizing that much foreign policy lies outside of treaties and observing the extent to which the American executive has acted upon its own responsibility in such matters, these advocates have sought to have the rule so framed as to embrace engagements of whatever nature. In 1921 M. Giolitti proposed a law in the Italian Parliament stipulating that treaties and "international understandings, whatever their subject and character," should be valid only after approval by Parliament;[11] but he retired from office before action was taken. By a resolution adopted at its annual conference in 1921, the British Labor party dissociated itself in advance from "any obligation towards foreign states which the British Government may have contracted, or may contract, in treaties, conventions, arrangements, or understandings of whatever nature, or for whatever purpose, which have not been submitted to or approved by Parliament."[12]

It is to be observed that, were such a constitutional provision established, it would still be a matter of

[10] Wright: *The control of American foreign relations*, p. 252.
[11] Morel: *Giolitti's bill to abolish secret diplomacy*, in *Foreign Affairs* (London), Jan., 1921.
[12] *Foreign Affairs* (London), July, 1921.

interpretation to determine what diplomatic acts of the many occurring daily constituted in fact an international understanding. The matter could obviously be carried to absurd and altogether impractical lengths. As it is, however, even the newest European constitutions leave the executive generally free with respect to political engagements.

The control which European parliaments may exercise over the executive conduct of foreign relations is derived, not primarily from constitutional restrictions, which are the hallmark of the American system, but from the operation of ministerial responsibility and from statutory control, more particularly the power of the purse.[13] Ministries have fallen frequently enough on questions of foreign policy to demonstrate the effectiveness of ministerial responsibility as a means of control whenever legislatures may care to exercise it. There is, however, the indifference of legislatures to external matters of which we have just now spoken, and there are said to be other difficulties. These difficulties, which are certainly to some extent real, relate to two main points, namely, first, the totality of policy, and second, the fact that in the realm of foreign affairs Parliament is frequently faced with accomplished facts which can be altered only at a disproportionate cost, if at all.

Under the first head arises a difficulty inherent in party government as applied to foreign relations. The domestic affairs of a state and its international relations are essentially different problems. The general attitude of a citizen or of a member of Par-

[13] *Cf.* Barthélemy: *Démocratie et la politique étrangère*, p. 132.

liament toward one need have little or nothing to do with his attitude toward the other. Yet foreign and domestic affairs are dealt with in the same party platforms and no means have been devised whereby an individual may support one party with respect to one of them and another party with respect to the other. There exists what Mr. Walter Lippmann has called the "false unity of political parties." "Men may agree on foreign politics," he wrote in 1915, "and disagree on domestic. But they have to vote wholesale while they think retail. The danger of this has been made evident by recent English history. For it is safe to say that the best Liberal thought was friendly to the internal policy of the Asquith government and hostile to its foreign policy. But the Liberals who wanted Lloyd-George had to swallow Sir Edward Grey and Winston Churchill. They could not change their diplomacy without wrecking their social reform."[14] In Parliament the political programmes of ministries must be accepted in their entirety.[15] Bryce remarks upon the difficulty of getting questions of foreign policy discussed in the British Parliament without regard to party ties.[16] This is so in every country, he adds, though the situation is accentuated in England where members of Parliament incline, even more than in other countries, to become merely the delegates of constituencies rather than their representatives.[17] As to the situation in France, where ministerial changes occur

[14] *The stakes of diplomacy*, p. 201.

[15] *Cf.* Lowell: *The government of England,* 1: 355.

[16] *International relations,* pp. 196-197. See also, in this connection, *Modern democracies,* 1: 117-118.

[17] *Modern democracies,* 2: 353.

154   THE CONDUCT OF FOREIGN RELATIONS

so readily, Barthélemy tells us that the majority in the French Chambers "asks only to approve with eyes closed the [foreign] policy of a ministry which embodies its fiscal, philosophical, religious, economic and social ideas."[18]

There should be mentioned as an offset to these difficulties the tendency of foreign policy to rise above party and take on a national character. Though partisan feeling has by no means been absent from the recent debates on foreign policy in the United States, it has been observed that party considerations do not usually have as much weight in the divisions on treaties in the Senate as in the consideration of questions of purely domestic concern.[19] Of the same import was the inclusion of both the majority and minority leaders of the Senate in the American delegation to the Conference on Limitation of Armament. A tendency may be observed in France also to hold foreign policy intact above the strife of parties[20] and ministers of foreign affairs have not infrequently held on longer than the cabinets to which they successively belonged.[21] A distinct separation of foreign policy from party politics has been brought about in England since 1890. This has been done deliberately in order to assure continuity of policy. Lord Rosebery said during a public address in 1895: "If there is one thing in my life I should like to have live after me, it is that, when I first went to the Foreign Office as Secretary for

[18] *Démocratie et la politique étrangère*, p. 136.
[19] *Cf.* Mathews: *The conduct of American foreign relations*, p. 163.
[20] Barthélemy, *op. cit.*, pp. 33 and 157.
[21] Chow, *op. cit.*, p. 204.

Foreign Affairs, I argued for and maintained the principle of continuity in foreign administration. My view was this, that whatever our domestic differences may be at home, we should preserve a united front abroad, and that foreign statesmen and foreign courts should feel that they are dealing, not with a ministry, possibly fleeting and possibly transient, but with a great, powerful, and united nation.'"[22]

Coming now to the difficulty that legislatures are sometimes faced with accomplished facts which cannot readily be altered, it should first be noted that the generality of members of any legislative body are uninformed concerning the detailed progress of the country's foreign relations and that this can hardly be different. A few, such as the members of a foreign relations committee, may be kept more or less *au courant*, but to keep all of several hundred legislators in touch with the day-to-day progress of diplomatic intercourse to an essentially greater extent than is now commonly done, even if it were practicable on the executive side,[23] would not really be

[22] Kennedy: *Old diplomacy and new*, p. 65.
[23] Speaking in the House of Commons, November 7, 1916, Sir Edward Carson said: "I think it would be well for the House to recollect that this question of giving more publicity to foreign negotiations—to diplomatic negotiations—is one that has been very often considered during the last fifty years or more. I have been twenty-four years in this House, and to my knowledge it has arisen on many occasions. But the truth of the matter is that nobody has ever been able to suggest a way in which the House and the country could at critical times get more information in regard to dealings with foreign questions without probably doing a great deal more harm than good. The responsibility must be with the Government—certainly while the War is going on, and as certainly during acute crises before a war. You must leave the responsibility with the Government, and the responsibility of this

welcome to the legislators themselves. They would have that much less time for the domestic concerns which make the first call upon their attention. Though undoubtedly there are foreign ministers and their assistants who fall into habits of undue reticence for one reason or another—frequently it is the sheer pressure of time—the general inclination nowadays is to keep the legislature and the country informed as far as practicable.[24] But the point of saturation may soon be reached. I venture the thought that the problem of the modern foreign minister, seeking legislative and popular support, is often how to get people to absorb more information rather than to keep information from them.

It is plain that the members of the legislature cannot all turn foreign secretary. The practical point is to determine the moment, in any particular transaction or episode, at which the essential facts may be laid before the legislature and the people. "The English constitutional system," according to Todd, "requires that Parliament should be informed, from time to time, of everything which is necessary to ex-

House is to take care that if that Government fails it shall no longer be trusted. I know of no other responsibility that this House has or can have." (*Parl. Debates, Commons*, 5th series, 67: 156.)

[24] Lord Robert Cecil said in the House of Commons, November 7, 1916: "I am very much in favor, if it could be devised, of some system which would enable the ministers of the Crown, particularly those connected with the Foreign Office, to give much more freely than they can do in debate in the House of Commons, the reasons for their policy, the difficulties they have had of all sorts which cannot even be alluded to in debate in public, and which cannot even be suggested in public, and to lay before their fellow-countrymen what their real case is." (*Parl. Debates, Commons*, 5th series, 87: 154.)

plain the conduct and policy of government, whether at home or abroad, in order that it may interpose with advice, assistance, or remonstrance, as the interests of the nation may appear to demand. . . . So long as Parliament is satisfied with the general principles upon which negotiations are being conducted, and approves of the general policy of the government, it should abstain from all interference with pending negotiations. . . . After the conclusion of important negotiations . . . it is usual for the government to communicate the result to Parliament, and to declare what is the course which the government proposes to take in regard to the question involved therein. If either House should be of opinion that the government has failed in its duty in any respect, it is competent for them to take any line of conduct they think proper, in order to make known to the crown their opinions upon the subject. For, while the initiation of a foreign policy is the prerogative of the crown, to be exercised under the responsibility of constitutional ministers, it is the duty of Parliament, when the result of the negotiations conducted by the ministers has been communicated to them, to criticise, support, or condemn that policy, as they may deem the interests of the nation shall require.''[25]

That was written more than half a century ago. Since then, as we have seen, it has come to be the frequent practice to lay information before Parliament even in the course of negotiations. The distinction still remains, however, and must remain, between the function of the legislature and the actual ad-

[25] *Parliamentary government in England,* 1: 601 and 612-613.

ministration of foreign affairs. "That is the real question," said Lord Grey in 1913, "which the House is raising when it talks about control over the Foreign Office, and it applies equally to other departments—to the Colonial Office and the India Office. This House is a deliberative body; it passes legislation, but it reviews policy and gives its approval or not, as the case may be. The House cannot really, by any arrangement of Committee, make itself into a real executive administrative body. It must be content with the position that the Cabinet is the real executive body responsible to Parliament to which the administration must be left, to be reviewed, however, by Parliament."[26] The foreign minister, the man who has the facts, must make the decisions and in this "restless world" decisions touching the relations of states often cannot wait. The foreign minister—to quote Lord Robert Cecil—"has to make up his mind, he has to send a telegram, he must decide and he cannot shift any part of that responsibility on to anybody else."[27] The inevitable result is that the legislature, when the facts are disclosed, sometimes finds itself in the presence of accomplished facts which can be altered only at a disproportionate cost, if at all.

It would be a grave error, however, to suppose that nowadays this is usually the case, or that the legislative department of any democratic government is without current influence on the course of foreign policy, or that parliaments, under that form of government, must precipitate a ministerial crisis in order to alter foreign policies. The main lines of

[26] Cited in Ponsonby, *op. cit.*, pp. 56 and 57.
[27] *Parl. Debates, Commons,* 5th series, 87: 151, Nov. 7, 1916.

policy must be generally understood and approved and a foreign minister must make his decisions not only in the light of his own judgment but with full regard to the movements of legislative and public opinion.[28] In England there is consultation from time to time with the leaders of the Opposition,[29] and it can hardly be doubted that in parliamentary governments generally the opinions held by the principal groups on all important points of foreign policy are known and weighed. Opinion transpires in debate. It is communicated privately. Groups and individual members do not hesitate to intervene with advice or orders when their interest is aroused. Immediately after Mr. Lloyd George disclosed to the press the gist of his conciliatory memorandum of March 25, 1919, concerning German reparations, 370 members of the Parliament which had been returned by the "khaki" election of 1918 despatched to him a telegram urging in the strongest terms that the financial claims of the Empire should be presented in full to Germany without consideration of Germany's capacity to pay, and so compelling was the despatch that he had to hasten back to London to reassure the House as to his intentions.[30]

[28] *Cf.* interview with Mr. Hughes in *McClure's Magazine* for July, 1923, pp. 12-13.
[29] See statement by Mr. Lambert, *Parl. Debates, Commons*, 5th series, 87: 150, Nov. 7, 1916; and Ponsonby, *op. cit.*, p. 35.
[30] Kennedy, *op. cit.*, p. 308; Baruch: *The making of the reparations and economic sections of the treaty*, p. 6.

A similar episode occurred in France in January, 1922, when in the midst of M. Briand's negotiations with Mr. Lloyd George at Cannes the French Senate Committee on Foreign Affairs telegraphed M. Briand a resolution by twenty-five Senators protesting against reductions in the reparations program and French partici-

Because such directives are not frequently imparted in so public a manner, their importance is, I believe, underrated. In the case of the United States, where the executive and legislative branches are to so great an extent mutually independent, it has been said that the President pursues foreign policies quite without control by Congress unless these "policies casually appear in treaties or require the passage of laws."[31] I do not believe that this is the case. All would agree that, where treaties are necessary, the constitutional authority of the Senate in that respect gives it an influence over the course of negotiation well in advance of the submission of the treaties for consent to ratification. The White House and State Department are constantly solicitous of senatorial desires and susceptibilities and shape their course of action under particular circumstances with one eye upon the exigencies of the situation itself and the other on Capitol Hill. With reference to the Panama treaty which he was negotiating with Sir Julian Pauncefote in 1899, Hay wrote Henry White, then our Chargé d'Affaires at London: "My principal purpose in drawing up the treaty was to avoid any contested points or anything which would cause acrimonious discussion in the Senate. I hope the Foreign Office will see with what sincere friendly purpose the treaty has been drawn, and will refrain from any changes or amendments, which, however meritorious in themselves, might cause the rejection

pation in the proposed Genoa Conference except upon certain conditions. M. Briand resigned soon afterwards. *Current History*, Feb., 1922, p. 867.

[31] *Cf.* Myers: *The control of foreign relations,* in *Am. Pol. Sci. Rev.,* 11: 41.

of the treaty by exciting the opposition of one-third of the Senate."[32] Senator Bacon said in 1906 that during his term in office it had been the practice of Presidents and Secretaries of State to confer with senators as to the propriety of negotiating or attempting to negotiate a treaty. "I know in my own experience," he said, "that it was the frequent practice of Secretary Hay, not simply after a proposed treaty had been negotiated, but before he had ever conferred with the representatives of the foreign power, to seek to have conference with Senators to know what they thought of such and such a proposition; and, if the subject-matter was a proper matter for negotiation, what senators thought as to certain provisions; and he advised with them as to what provisions should be incorporated."[33]

This informal contact, which grows and diminishes with the variations of personality and politics, has also its influence in that domain of foreign policy, well known to be large, which lies beyond the pale of treaties. Consider for example the question of the recognition of new governments. Here the President's power is constitutionally unrestricted, but it is not to be doubted that the prevailing sentiment in Congress, as informally ascertained, is a constant and influential factor in determining his course of action in particular cases. I am convinced that the presidential policy of the last decade with respect to Mexico, and later with respect to Russia, could not have been maintained if it had not had the support of a preponderating opinion in Congress. If

[32] Thayer: *Life and letters of John Hay*, 2: 216 and 217.
[33] Cited in Corwin: *The President's control of foreign relations*, p. 186; and Wright, *op. cit.*, pp. 250 and 251.

this is true under the presidential form of government, it should be plain that in parliamentary governments, where the ministry of the day leads so hazardous an existence, the executive can act in important external matters only with the general approbation of a majority in Parliament. I believe that knowledge of this fact is one of the reasons why European constitution-makers, even in the newest and most radical countries, have been willing to leave to the executive so great a constitutional latitude with respect to the conduct of foreign relations.

In the United States knowledge of the sentiments of Congress obtained through informal contact is supplemented by congressional resolutions. These resolutions, touching upon every phase of foreign policy, have been so numerous that they are now familiar facts. While they are not mandatory, as they would probably be in Great Britain,[34] they exert at times a decided influence on executive policy.[35] The Senate resolution of January 6, 1923, recommending the withdrawal of the American troops from the Rhine,[36] may be called to mind, and it is interesting to find in a recent interview with Mr. Hughes touching, among other matters, the pending question of American participation in the World Court, reference to a concurrent resolution of 1890 recommending to the executive the making of arrangements for the peaceful settlement of international disputes.[37]

There remains, in addition to the influence which

[34] Bryce: *American commonwealth*, 1: 211 *n*.
[35] *Cf*. Corwin, *op. cit*., p. 45.
[36] *Cong. Rec.*, Jan. 6, 1923, p. 1383.
[37] *McClure's Magazine*, July, 1923, p. 14.

legislatures derive from the political coördination of the two departments of government, the second general means of control mentioned above, namely, statutory control, including the power of the purse. Laws are needed to give effect to many international engagements which are not constitutionally subject to legislative approval. The Declaration of London of 1909, an international pact codifying the laws of naval warfare, was duly signed by the British delegates; but the royal ratification was perforce withheld because the House of Lords rejected the bill which was introduced in Parliament for the purpose of giving effect to the provisions of the pact. The pact then became a dead letter, although it had already been approved for ratification by the Senate of the United States and other signatory powers had taken steps to promulgate and enforce it.[38] The French executive was constitutionally competent to conclude an alliance with Russia calling for joint military action in certain contingencies, but recourse had to be had in 1913 to the French Chambers to obtain an extension of the period of compulsory military service to three years.[39]

The situation is somewhat different in the United States because, in distinction to England and France,[40] treaties are part of the supreme law of the land and are to some extent self-executing. It follows, however, from this very fact that they may be abrogated by subsequent enactments of Congress,

[38] *Am. Jour. Int. Law,* 1915, p. 199.
[39] Chow, *op. cit.,* p. 179. See Chow, pp. 179-185, as to treaties, not included in Article 8 of the French constitution, but requiring legislative action nevertheless to give them effect.
[40] *Cf.* Chow, *op. cit.,* pp. 267-269.

and treaties which require the appropriation of money or affect the fiscal policy of the Government are kept closely dependent upon legislative action.[41]

Bryce expresses the opinion that under the American system the power of the purse gives Congress less control over the President than European parliaments may exercise by the same means over their executives. Congress can check any particular scheme which the President favors by refusing supplies for it, but Congress cannot coerce him within the limits of his constitutional functions in the same way that the British House of Commons might coerce a ministry by refusing supplies altogether. There is only the rather lame expedient of "riders" to appropriation bills.[42] Mr. Hughes said recently: "The Congress, of course, controls the purse, but in the case of the constitutional authority of the executive, as in that of the Supreme Court exercising the judicial power, the duty of the Congress to furnish the money needed for the essential equipment to exercise the authority has always been recognized."[43]

Yet the American Congress has gone far in its use of the fiscal prerogative. In the early days of the government the President was unhampered by the terms of the appropriations for foreign representation. So much money was voted "for the expenses of foreign intercourse," to be expended at the discretion of the President. No mention was made of ministers of a specified grade at this or that place.[44] Today the appropriation acts are

[41] *Cf.* Mathews, *op. cit.,* pp. 206 ff.
[42] Bryce: *American commonwealth,* 1: 213-214.
[43] *Am. Jour. Int. Law,* July, 1922, p. 355.
[44] Corwin, *op. cit.,* pp. 66-67.

minutely particular, specifying the grades of the diplomatic representatives which are to be appointed and the places to which they may be sent. On September 4, 1913, for example, an act was passed authorizing the President to appoint an ambassador to Spain, who should receive as compensation so much per annum,[45] though the actual appropriation of the money was made separately in the general deficiency bill of that year.[46] The constitutional effectiveness of such statutes may be questionable,[47] but so far they have in fact governed the action of the executive in making the diplomatic appointments in question. A very striking example of encroachment may be observed in the deficiency appropriation act of 1913, which embodied this provision: "Hereafter the Executive shall not extend or accept any invitation to participate in any international congress, conference, or like event, without first having specific authority of law to do so."[48] It is practically certain that this attempted restriction could not withstand the test of constitutionality. The President called the Conference on Limitation of Armament without reference to congressional action.[49]

Fiscal control is most important in connection with war. Here its power is absolute. The sinews of war can be had only from legislatures. The American, French, and many other constitutions vest the power to declare war in the legislature, but even in

[45] 38 *Stat. L.* 110.
[46] 38 *Stat. L.* 312.
[47] *Cf.* Corwin, *op. cit.*, p. 70.
[48] 37 *Stat. L.* 913.
[49] *Cf.* remarks by Senator Borah and others in *Cong. Rec.*, Dec. 27, 1922, pp. 939-940.

Great Britain, where this right lies exclusively with the Crown, "to be exercised according to the discretion of the sovereign, as he may judge the honour and interests of the nation to require,"[50] the power of the purse places it within the effective control of Parliament, as English kings discovered as long ago as Charles II. "The question of peace or war has always been in the control of the House of Commons," said Lord Grey in 1911, ". . . It is absolutely impossible for any government to contemplate war unless it feels certain that when the moment comes the House of Commons would be prepared to endorse the policy of the government by voting the supplies which are necessary and without which it would be absolutely out of the power of the government to go to war at all."[51]

This view is combated by an Irish member of Parliament, Mr. Swift MacNeill, who reverts to the old difficulty of the accomplished fact. "When the nation has embarked in war," he writes, "the idea of cutting off the supplies for the army or of in any way taking any step calculated to imperil the efficiency of the army as a fighting force is unthinkable."[52] This does not stand analysis. As President Lowell has pointed out, there are two kinds of wars—those that do not threaten the security of the state and those that do.[53] In the first category of wars adverse criticism of the Government is tolerated. The legisla-

[50] Todd, *op. cit.*, 1: 598. According to Chow (p. 55) the constitutions of Belgium, Holland, Italy, and Spain also, like that of Great Britain, vest the war power in the executive.
[51] *Parl. Debates, Commons,* 5th series, 24: 538-539.
[52] *Parliament and foreign policy* (London, 1917), p. 7.
[53] *Public opinion in war and peace,* pp. 228 ff.

ture may act to bring such wars to an end despite the wishes of the executive. The intervention of the House of Commons to end the war against the American colonies[54] may be recalled, as well as the open opposition in England to the Crimean and Boer wars. On the other hand, when a war threatens the existence of the state no derogation from the national effort is tolerated. Then it is that Mr. MacNeill's remark is applicable, but under the circumstances it becomes only the complaint of a hopeless minority. The intolerance which forbids stinting of legislative support but reflects the conviction of the vast majority that the state is threatened and their determination to prosecute the war with the utmost energy. Thus, in the case of secondary wars or military expeditions which may not be regarded as wars in a constitutional sense, the legislature retains full control by reason of the necessity which the executive is under to seek appropriations at frequent intervals. Into wars of the first magnitude a modern democratic state may not be precipitated without full agreement on the subject between the executive and a large majority in the legislature.

How essential this agreement is manifests itself in an interesting way. In Great Britain, where the right to declare war is vested by the constitution in the Crown, the practical control is generally stated to rest with Parliament, while in the United States, where the same right is vested constitutionally in Congress, the authoritative statement is made that the war power rests actually in the hands of the President.[55] Mathews asserts that Congress has

[54] Todd, *op. cit.*, 1: 599.
[55] Pomeroy: *Constitutional law,* p. 565, cited in Corwin, *op. cit.,* pp. 130 and 131.

never, on the one hand, declared war except in pursuance of at least a virtual recommendation by the President, nor, on the other hand, refused a declaration when so recommended.[56] The significance of this appears to be that in modern democratic states the war-making power—so far as concerns wars of the first order which do not admit domestic opposition—vests not in the executive or the legislative branch as may be ordained by the constitution, but has its only being in a national conviction so unmistakable that the spokesmen of the people in both departments of government agree in proclaiming it.

Here is an epitome indeed of the whole question of the control of foreign relations. Foreign policy is the expression of the international aspirations of a people. Its fundamentals are determined by the particular circumstances of their existence. For practical reasons the detailed development of policy must be committed to the hands of a few, chosen for the purpose from time to time. The larger group to whom legislation is entrusted, or the whole people, have effective means of control. It is only as they become preoccupied with other matters that the few may lead policy into ways that do not command general approval. When interest is aroused, when the public attention becomes focused upon particular situations, the executive can proceed only with full public support. When a national war befalls, it is not one department that acts. The whole government must move in accord.[57]

[56] *The conduct of American foreign relations*, pp. 257 ff.
[57] *Cf.* the following description by Professor Myers of the British decision to enter the war in 1914: "Statements by both the secretary of state for foreign affairs and the prime minister

were made to parliament before the act, and these were notably accurate, as a textual comparison with the entire set of diplomatic documents published subsequently will indicate. Sir Edward Grey closed by saying: 'If . . . we are forced . . . to take our stand upon those issues, then I believe, when the country realizes what is at stake, what the real issues are . . . we shall be supported throughout, not only by the house of commons, but by the determination, the resolution, the courage and the endurance of the whole country.' No opposition was voiced. The leader of the party out of power, Bonar Law, assured the government that 'they can rely on the unhesitating support of the opposition.' The Irish leader reiterated the same sentiment. Many speakers voiced hopes that the government would not push toward war and would find a way to maintain peace, but these members all seemed to agree with one of their number, Ramsay Macdonald, who referred to 'a house which in a great majority is with him [Sir Edward Grey].' And the essence of parliamentary government is that a majority takes decisions and gives mandates. The next day (August 4), the Prime Minister announced the circumstances and the fact of the ultimatum, again without opposition." *Legislatures and foreign relations,* in *Am. Pol. Sci. Rev.,* 11: 673 and 674.

CHAPTER X

CRYSTALLIZATION AND ENFORCEMENT OF OPINION THROUGH OTHER CHANNELS

THE crystallization and enforcement of public opinion with respect to foreign affairs may take place not only through the legislature but also through the press, through political parties and elections, and in a number of general ways.

The influence of the press is exercised through the editorial formulation of opinion and through the manner of presenting the news. It is difficult to estimate in any general way the effect of editorial opinion, but it is an indubitable factor at times in the determination of policy. Thus we read in a London press despatch of December 10, 1922, that Premier Poincaré, then at the British capital, asserted that France would demand the occupation of the Ruhr as a fundamental guarantee for any moratorium and that he reasserted this demand after receiving advices from Paris that his attitude in London had been interpreted in the Chamber of Deputies and by a portion of the press as a weakening in the face of Mr. Bonar Law.[1]

Writers of "leaders" in certain European papers, such as M. André Tardieu in the Paris *Temps*, enjoy a considerable authority. Editorials in the American press have lost the element of personal influence which was common in the time of Horace Greeley and have become analyses of the news and

[1] Washington *Post*, Dec. 11, 1922.

comments thereon from the point of view of a particular community or of a newspaper which as an institution maintains certain political and other traditions. Editorials of this kind have great value as mirrors of crystallizing opinion. They are gathered up by many agencies and reproduced in periodicals devoted to the purpose. It is probably the case that at least one periodical summary of editorial opinion is read with some regularity and thoroughness by every important official in this country, as well as by editors and others concerned with the development of opinion, and the same is no doubt the case in other democracies.

The importance of the press in connection with the crystallization of public opinion on foreign affairs rests less, however, upon the influence of views editorially expressed than upon the latitude which may be employed in the presentation of the news. The function of newspapers as the great disseminators of information in this field is not merely mechanical. Entirely aside from conscious or unconscious coloring, which is also frequently present, there must be selection of facts and choice of emphasis, and these may have the most decided influence upon the immediate public reaction to the situations described. This is well understood by those who conduct the foreign affairs of democracies. Describing the position of the newspaper correspondents at Paris, Mr. Baker recounts that while there was "a gesture of unconcern, of don't-care-what-they-say," on the part of some of the delegates, "no aspect of the Conference in reality worried them more than the news, opinions, guesses, that went out by scores of thousands of words every night, and the reactions which came back so promptly from them."[2]

The importance which the press has attained in this way has not failed indeed to elicit in England manifestations of parliamentary jealousy. Criticizing Mr. Lloyd George's conduct of affairs at the Genoa Conference, a prominent member of the House of Lords said: "I cannot help expressing what I believe all your Lordships would feel— namely, that it would be happier for us if the Prime Minister felt that he was accountable to Parliament and to Parliament alone, and not to the Press anywhere, and that the whole object of information is to provide something for the permanent guidance of Parliament, and not headlines for the newspapers next day."[3]

It has even been suggested that "newspapers and the capacity of the constituent masses to read them have sapped the foundations of representative government."[4] But with respect to foreign affairs there is a controlling factor to be kept in mind. The ability of the press to influence public opinion in particular directions is restricted by the number and variety of the newspapers which deal with matters of such general concern. The situation is essentially different from what it is in the field of local affairs where the interested public may be limited to an area in which a single newspaper dominates. Even

[2] *Woodrow Wilson and the world settlement,* 1:117.
[3] *Parl. Debates, Lords,* 5th series, 51:6, June 27, 1922. For an earlier complaint by a member of the House of Commons, see *Parl. Debates, Commons,* 5th series, 87:154.
[4] See McBain and Rogers: *The new constitutions of Europe,* p. 22, and the references given there.

the ability of newspapers to influence the initial trend of opinion by coloring or emphasis in the presentation of the news is to some extent neutralized in the case of foreign affairs by the inevitable variety of the coloring and emphasis. When it comes to the editorial interpretation of the news, political partisanship and the natural variety of editorial minds go far to assure the statement of every important point of view.

The fact is that, while the press is a factor of the very first importance in the crystallization of opinion with respect to foreign affairs, its power to enforce opinion on particular issues is not so great as it is sometimes thought to be. Particular papers may acquire weight in the formulation of policy. The position of the London *Times* during the latter half of the last century is well remembered, but its authority was largely due to current understanding with the officials of the Foreign Office, and somewhat the same might be said of the Paris *Temps*. A string of papers may be built up as Mr. Hearst has done in the United States, but it has always seemed to me that the remarkable thing about the Hearst papers, considering their great numerical distribution and the intelligent organization back of them, is the comparatively slight influence which they seem able to exert in particular directions, though their general influence among some sections of the population in fostering international distrust is no doubt considerable. The recent trial of strength between Lord Northcliffe and Mr. Lloyd George was a most illuminating demonstration of the limits of the power of the press to dominate executive action. It is said to have been Northcliffe's avowed intention to govern England, including the foreign relations of England, through the use of his papers. Certainly he was in a strong position, but all the prestige of the London *Times,* the influence of his other publications, and his own determination and forceful intelligence did not avail to bring him even within reach of his ambitious purpose.

It is interesting to observe in connection with the function of the press that the development of opinion on particular subjects constitutes news and is duly reported as such by the papers. In the despatches telling of the latest reparations note given out at London, for example, we read not only of the note itself but of its effect upon different sections of the British public, and in the next column we may find a despatch from Paris, and possibly others from Brussels, Rome, and Berlin, telling of its reception at those capitals. The press performs a valuable service in this way, for the general result must be to foster broader and fairer views of international problems and to favor the development of those cosmopolitan currents of thought, often potent factors for good, which go to make up what we call the public opinion of the world.

Public opinion on foreign affairs finds expression also through political parties and elections, but not very satisfactorily. We have already referred to the "false unity" of political parties with respect to foreign and domestic issues.[5] Issues of foreign policy are drawn into the arena of domestic politics, become the playthings of party strife, and are seldom dealt with on their merits alone. In the Canadian

[5] *Supra,* p. 153.

election of 1911 the Conservative party came into power by distorting the proposal for tariff reciprocity with the United States into a purpose on the part of the latter to annex Canada. John Hay wrote Choate in 1899, with some partisan spirit himself: "The Democratic press evidently thinks there is some political capital to be made by denouncing any arrangement with England, and they, in common with a large number of German newspapers, are ready to attack any treaty with England, no matter how advantageous to us, as a hostile act towards Ireland and Germany. The Democratic Convention of Iowa has adopted . . . resolutions in this sense, which seem too ridiculous to treat seriously; but all these senseless charges indicate the intention of the opposition to make a party matter of our relations with England, and to oppose any treaty we may make with that country."[6]

The incompatibility of party government with the unity of the state as an international person has given rise to a strong tendency, which we have already observed, to lift foreign policy above partisan conflict. This is most marked when foreign relations are vital. Since the foundation of the Third Republic the general lines of French foreign policy have been determined by its position toward Germany. All parties have felt alike on this supreme issue of national safety and all have agreed in keeping it out of party controversy, with the result that incessant changes of ministries have scarcely touched the continuity of foreign policy.[7] In England, as we have

[6] Thayer: *John Hay*, 2: 218; see also the letters on pp. 220-221.
[7] *Modern democracies*, 2: 372. See also Thomas, T. H.: *Political parties and foreign policy in France*, in *World's Work*, 43: 146-

seen, there has been a deliberate effort since 1890 to have politics "stop at the seashore."

Issues of foreign policy have so far had a very small part in American party politics. According to an authority on our party system, there have been four broad party divisions since the Government was founded. In only one of these, the first, has there been a clear issue of foreign policy. This was in the division between Federalists and Democrats, when of four main issues one was the question of the policy to be pursued toward revolutionary France. The second broad division, between Democrats and Whigs, and the third, between Democrats and Republicans, involved no important external issues whatever. In the fourth or present party division there have emerged only the uncertain issue of imperialism in 1900 and that of the League of Nations in 1920.[8]

References to foreign affairs in our party platforms have been to a great extent mere political catchpennies. Often they are identical on both sides. Both the Republican and Democratic platforms of 1888 mentioned sympathy with Ireland; those of 1892, opposition to the Czar, friendliness for Ireland, and the Nicaragua Canal. The Republican platform favored the extension of foreign commerce. In 1896 there was the same absence of any real foreign issue. Of three points of divergence in 1900, one, under the slogan of imperialism, touched foreign policy, namely, the course to be pursued with respect to the Philippine Islands. The Democrats contended

150, Dec., 1921, and Margaine, A.: *La politique extérieure de la France et le parti radical*, in *Nouvelle Revue*, Dec. 1, 1921.

[8] Merriam: *The American party system*, chap. viii.

that this was the "paramount issue," while the Republicans insisted that the real issue was the currency. There was nothing of note in the following four campaigns. In 1920 the platforms of both parties agreed substantially in planks regarding the merchant marine, Mexico, and sympathy with Armenia. Special planks in the Democratic platform included sympathy with Ireland, China, the Czecho-Slovaks, Finland, Poland, and Persia, together with some particular mention of the Philippines, Porto Rico, Hawaii, and Alaska. The only important difference was on the question of the League of Nations, and here the issue was not clearly drawn and the meaning of the result of the election remains a matter of dispute.[9]

Besides 1900 and 1920, I know of only two other elections in the United States which were important with respect to foreign policy—those of 1810 and 1844. The congressional elections of 1810 returned the "war hawks" and, together with the state election in Massachusetts in the following spring, crystallized the belligerent spirit which had been aroused by the oppression of American rights in the preceding years and opened the way for the outbreak of hostilities with England.[10] In 1844 the Democrats declared emphatically for the annexation of Texas, and the campaign was conducted on "the plain and attractive issue of expansion." Other differences were largely neutralized by hedging on both sides, and the people were allowed to vote "more strictly on a single issue than is usually the case in a national

[9] Merriam: *The American party system*, chap. viii.
[10] Adams, Henry: *History of the United States during the first administration of Madison*, vol. 2, chaps. vi and vii.

election, and no doubt could remain that the country desired annexation." Back of the external question of annexation lay, of course, the domestic problem of slavery, which had appeared now for the first time as an important factor in a national election. It is interesting to note that, the decision for annexation having been taken at the polls, consummation did not wait upon Polk's induction into office, but was brought about by joint resolution of Congress March 1, 1845, upon the recommendation of Tyler, who called the attention of Congress to the manifestation of the popular will.[11]

Of English elections in modern democratic times only those of 1857 and 1880 can be said to have turned clearly upon questions of foreign policy. In the former year the action of a British official in China in the affair of the lorch *Arrow* led to hostilities and roused a sudden and sharp controversy. The House of Commons passed a resolution of censure upon the official's conduct, and the Ministry, which supported him, appealed to the country and obtained a majority by a campaign in which the "insult to the flag" argument was effectively used.[12] The election of 1880 was a duel between Disraeli and Gladstone over the general character of the external policy to be pursued by Great Britain. In a speech at West Calder April 2 Gladstone defined in general terms six "right principles of foreign policy." He succeeded to power for five years as a result of the campaign and gave specific effect to those principles

[11] Fish, C. R.: *The development of American nationality*, pp. 305-307.

[12] Bryce: *Modern democracies*, 2: 377; Myers: *Legislatures and foreign relations*, in *Am. Pol. Sci. Rev.*, 11: 672-673.

by a number of measures, which included withdrawal from Afghanistan, from the Sudan, and from the Transvaal.[13] This is possibly the best instance in which party government enabled the electorate to make a choice between two clearly opposed courses of foreign policy. It should be noted that Gladstone was not altogether successful in realizing the principles on which he had stood and disappointed his more ardent supporters by the retention of Cyprus and by his policy in Egypt.[14]

Foreign affairs naturally enter much more largely in England than in the United States into current politics. In August, 1898, the government of the day received a notable warning in a by-election in Lancashire, where the Radical candidate who won made an issue of the timidity of Lord Salisbury's policy in China. It was charged that Russia and France had scored successes at the expense of British finance and that British commerce in the Far East, a matter of direct interest to the Lancashire operatives, would suffer in consequence.[15] The general elections of 1900 and 1905 turned more or less upon British policy in South Africa, but these elections more than anything else demonstrated the difficulty of diagnosing the suffrages of the people with regard to particular issues. "In England," according to President Lowell, "where of late years a doctrine has grown up that Parliament ought to enact no drastic legislation without a mandate from the nation, a general election always gives rise to a dispute about the questions it has decided. Did the people in 1900 de-

[13] Kennedy: *Old diplomacy and new,* pp. 47-48.
[14] *Cf.* Rose, J. Holland: *The rise of democracy,* p. 246.
[15] Kennedy, *op. cit.,* p. 84.

clare for anything but the South African war? At the election of 1905, which brought the Liberals into power, did the people pronounce in favor of secular schools, or Home Rule for Ireland, or merely against a preferential tariff?" "A general election," he continues, "is of necessity a judgment upon the parties in all their relations, and therefore it is impossible to isolate the different motives involved, such as the personal qualities of the candidates, the various measures proposed, and a revulsion of feeling against the party in power. One cannot separate these things so as to attribute the result to any one of them alone. That is the chief reason for taking a popular vote on a single measure by means of a referendum."[16]

The referendum has not been extensively tried in connection with foreign affairs. None of the revolutionary constitutions of France, not even that of 1793, submitted treaties to popular vote, though under the constitution of 1793 a declaration of war might be so controlled.[17] As we have seen, the new constitutions of Europe which provide for plebiscites expressly except foreign affairs from their operation. Article 34 of the Esthonian constitution, which may be taken as typical, reads: "The budget, the raising of loans, income tax laws, declaration of war and the making of peace, declaration of a state of defense and termination of same, declaration of mobilization and demobilization, as well as treaties with foreign states, are not subject to a plebiscite and cannot be decided by a plebiscite."

[16] *Public opinion and popular government*, pp. 73-75.
[17] Barthélemy: *Démocratie et la politique étrangère*, pp. 124 and 125.

A referendum was conducted in Switzerland in May, 1920, to determine whether that country should join the League of Nations. About three-quarters of the electorate voted, which is a high proportion, though not the highest on record. Racial, linguistic, religious, and personal prejudices cut across party lines to a considerable extent. The result was favorable by a substantial popular majority, but the vote by cantons was very close. The French and Italian parts of Switzerland strongly favored the League, while German-speaking Switzerland gave a majority against it.[18]

In January, 1921, Switzerland accepted by a decisive vote a constitutional amendment in the following terms: "Treaties with foreign powers which are concluded without limit of time or for a period of more than fifteen years shall also be submitted to the people for acceptance or rejection upon demand of 30,000 Swiss citizens qualified to vote, or of eight cantons." The movement in favor of this constitutional change is said to have had its origin in popular indignation resulting from disclosures in 1909 of a secret transaction in connection with the St. Gotthard Treaty. Final action was delayed by the war until 1921.[19] The first referendum on a treaty was conducted in February, 1923, and resulted in the defeat of an agreement signed in 1919 by France and Switzerland readjusting a frontier customs district in the region of Savoy which had been established by the Treaty of Vienna of 1815. The vote against the treaty was four to one, although the population of Geneva, the only part of the Swiss population said

[18] *Am. Pol. Sci. Rev.*, Aug., 1920, p. 477.
[19] *Ibid.*, Aug., 1921, p. 423.

to be really interested, declared for it. I have been told that the vote was influenced by racial prejudice and that the merits of the matter had small weight. The French Government has declined to concur in the rejection of the agreement on the ground that it was concluded before the Swiss constitutional amendment was adopted, and it was reported in the press last May that feeling had been engendered between the two countries.[20] It cannot be said that the experiment has so far proved a success. The special position of Switzerland and the simplicity of its foreign policy must also be kept in mind.

The obstacles in the way of using the referendum in connection with foreign affairs are obvious. Aside from the difficulty created by the swift movement of events, it is usually impossible to state clear and unqualified alternatives. If some foreign power interfered intolerably with American commerce on the high seas and war seemed the only alternative, the submission of the bald question of peace or war to the people would either preclude the possibility of an eleventh-hour adjustment or expose the country fatally to military attack. If the question asked were whether there should be war unless the President were able to reach a "satisfactory adjustment" in the meantime, the matter would be effectively left in the President's hands, where it was originally. A national referendum on the League issue was proposed recently, and it was suggested that this form of question be used: "Shall the United States become a member of the League of Nations, upon such reservations or amendments to the covenant of the

[20] *Living Age,* May 5, 1923, and New York *Times,* Feb. 4 and 19, 1923.

League as the Senate of the United States, with the approval of the President, may agree upon?"[21] It is difficult to see how an affirmative vote on this question would decide the issue.

If formal referenda on questions of foreign policy are impracticable, there are still numerous ways, outside the official machinery, by which the attitude of the public or of sections of it toward particular problems finds expression. Unofficial organizations, among them labor bodies and chambers of commerce, concern themselves on occasion with questions of foreign relations. A notable instance occurred in England in August, 1920, when the Labour Council of Action threatened Mr. Lloyd George that any steps taken in favor of Poland against Soviet Russia, whose armies were then threatening Warsaw, would be resisted by "any and every form of withdrawal of labor which circumstances may require."[22] "Direct action" of this kind, defying or setting aside constitutional expedients, is fortunately rare. The more usual, and very useful, function of these bodies is to ascertain and make known the sentiment of their membership with respect to the matters in which they are interested. The American Federation of Labor has recently done a valuable public service in crystallizing the preponderant view of labor in this country on the subject of the recognition of the Soviet régime in Russia. The Chamber of Commerce of the United States conducts referenda among its

[21] Lucking, Alfred: *A national vote on the League,* in *Our World,* May, 1923.
[22] Lowell: *Public opinion in war and peace,* p. 263; Kennedy, *op. cit.,* pp. 334-335.

membership on important public questions, including questions of foreign relations, and maintains a standing committee on foreign affairs for the current consideration of such matters. In October last the chambers of commerce in 160 of the principal cities of France were asked by some of their number to express an opinion as to the advisability of resuming commercial relations with Russia. It appeared at one time that the decision would be favorable and that the chambers would despatch an economic mission to Moscow, but apparently a different view developed later and the project was dropped.[23]

The number of unofficial organizations which interest themselves in foreign relations, either in a general way or from a special angle, is growing. The opinions which they elicit are often helpful to responsible officials in determining the trend of public thought, but it is not always easy to know how representative or disinterested they are. Former Senator Husting of Wisconsin testified that during the months previous to America's entry into the war, the German-American Alliance sent thousands of telegrams urging a conciliatory policy toward Germany, until it appeared that such was the overwhelming demand of his constituents. Those whose only interest was the general welfare of America very rarely expressed to him their beliefs, although, upon investigation, he became convinced that they were in the vast majority.[24]

State legislatures in the United States, which have no official competence in the realm of foreign affairs, nevertheless give expression to their views respect-

[23] New York *Times*, Oct. 22, 1922.
[24] Hall, A. B.: *Popular government,* pp. 60 and 61.

ing particular matters. A number of them recently adopted resolutions on the subject of the recognition of Mexico. A resolution of the Ohio Senate advocating the adherence of the United States to the World Court elicited from President Harding last March an appreciative acknowledgment in which he set forth at some length his view of the matter.[25]

Individual citizens, acting sometimes spontaneously and sometimes at the inspiration of those more particularly interested, make known their views to the executive, in personal interviews or more frequently in letters and petitions. Members of the legislative branch, as the personal representatives of their constituents, may be asked to intervene.

Probably the most remarkable instance of a widespread and direct manifestation of opinion occurred during the Washington Conference on the Limitation of Armament. The Committee of General Information of the Advisory Council of the American Delegation, which handled the communications which citizens and organizations all over the United States addressed to the delegation on the subject of the work of the Conference, estimated that up to January 15, 1922, it had heard from 13,878,671 persons, or say one-tenth of the population of the country. The opinions expressed related to all aspects of the work of the Conference. It is interesting to note that an overwhelming majority (11,642,685), while advocating in general terms the coöperative limitation of armament, favored leaving to the discretion of the delegates the extent of the restrictions to be

[25] New York *Times*, Feb. 3, 1923, editorial, *Working for Mexico;* ibid., March 6, 1923. See also Mathews: *The conduct of American foreign relations*, p. 33.

imposed. Two hundred and seventy-one thousand nine hundred and twenty-six favored limitation with "benevolence and liberality," 29,919 demanded complete disarmament, 12,798 declared against any limitation, 11,647 advised caution in arranging the limitation, and 8,454 demanded an increase in naval strength.[26]

Public opinion upon pending issues may be canvassed by magazines as a matter of editorial or business enterprise—for example, the poll of sentiment on the League of Nations taken by the *Literary Digest*. *L'Opinion,* a Paris weekly, printed in its issues of last autumn the replies of prominent French statesmen and publicists to three questions relating to the restoration of Europe and a possible revision of the Treaty of Versailles. A summary of these expressions was reproduced in this country in the *Living Age* of December 30, 1922, pages 730-732.

The public sometimes reacts promptly and definitely to exigent foreign situations as they arise; and there is no mistaking the nature of the sentiment, which asserts itself in a multiplicity of ways. After the Turks had massacred a large number of Bulgarians in 1876, the Czar summoned the Sultan to introduce certain reforms, and upon his refusal to do so proceeded to declare war. Bryce recounts that "Lord Beaconsfield, who was then at the head of the British Government, did not conceal his sympathy with the Turks, and would probably have carried Britain into a war against Russia to defend them had not an agitation in the country, which had been

[26] New York *Times,* Jan. 18, 1922, also issues of Dec. 12, 17, and 19, 1921.

shocked by the news of the massacre, deterred his Cabinet from that course."[27]

The executive may take the initiative in sounding public opinion on an uncertain issue, as illustrated by the following extract from a London press despatch of January 24, 1923: "The question of the withdrawal of the British troops from Cologne came into added prominence today through a statement in the *Evening Standard* that Prime Minister Bonar Law was sufficiently undecided about it to take steps to sound public opinion in different parts of the country. He has discovered, it is also affirmed, that public opinion in London and the South generally is mainly in favor of France, but that there is a distinct desire for withdrawal from the Rhine in Lancashire among both employers and workers. It is, of course, quite likely that the Premier has his ear to the ground and is listening as closely as possible to every whisper of popular sentiment. That is the business of a Prime Minister in times of such difficulty as the present."[28]

By all these means the officials who are responsible for the conduct of the foreign relations of democratic countries are kept informally in contact with sentiment and alive to the national and individual interests involved in particular matters that arise. There is a disposition among some who have discussed the democratic control of foreign relations to overlook this direct relationship as well as the representative character of the executive branch.[29] It is

[27] *Modern democracies*, 2: 378.
[28] New York *Times*, Jan. 25, 1923.
[29] As an instance to the contrary, see Myers: *Legislatures and foreign relations*, in *Am. Pol. Sci. Rev.*, 11: 672.

especially important to bear in mind that the chief of state, personifying the national tradition, may often give form and validity to the deeper currents of popular instinct in a way that no other organ of government can do. I believe that this underlies the influence which the British sovereign may at times exercise upon the course of foreign policy. The position of the President of the United States, who is both chief of state and prime minister, is very clearly that of national leader and spokesman, to whom the people may turn in crises for the expression of their inarticulate thought and feeling. To a remarkable degree the American presidents have embodied the mentality and character of the people in their best forms, and when a crisis arises they can usually be trusted to do what the "average citizen" would have done, if he had known how to do it, more certainly than a popular assembly. Mr. Walter Lippmann describes graphically the feeling of confidence in Mr. Wilson the day after the *Lusitania* was destroyed and the wish of those anxious for peace that Congress should not be summoned but the situation left in his hands.[30] Professor Philip Marshall Brown, remarking upon the great confidence which the American people repose in their President in the conduct of foreign relations and the non-partisan manner in which they rally to his support upon occasion, cites the public attitude at the time of the occupation of Vera Cruz by American forces in April, 1914, and recalls also "how, at the time of the crisis with Germany over the sinking of the *Sussex*, when certain interests opposed to the policy of the Presi-

[30] *The stakes of diplomacy*, chap. i.

dent endeavored to curb his freedom by Congressional action, the whole country indignantly warned Congress to leave the control of foreign relations . . . in the hands of the President and his advisers."[31]

The President may stand at times against the more manifest and superficial currents of public sentiment and hold the country to a course which its solid and less vocal common sense in the end approves. Professor Brown recalls that Washington "was compelled to face a most trying situation at the time of the French Revolution, when many Americans—Jefferson included—felt strongly convinced that the United States was bound by its Treaty of Alliance with France to come to its aid against Great Britain. Washington, however, with as keen a sense of honor, but with a wider range of vision, a realization of all the factors involved, and an appreciation of the permanent best interests of the United States, wisely determined otherwise. As DeTocqueville justly observes, 'nothing but the inflexible character of Washington, and the immense popularity which he enjoyed, could have prevented the Americans from declaring war against England. . . . The majority reprobated his policy, but it was afterward approved by the whole nation.' "

[31] *International realities,* p. 184.

CHAPTER XI

EFFECTIVENESS AND EFFICIENCY

Is there effective democratic control of the executive conduct of foreign relations in the countries which we have studied? I believe that we have found that there are effective means of control. Let us review the constitutional situation in the United States, Great Britain, and France. These countries exemplify the principal forms in which democratic government has so far been put in operation on a large scale and display at the same time the varying conditions of international existence. The United States maintains congressional or presidential government; Great Britain, parliamentary government under an hereditary monarchy; and France, parliamentary government under a republic. The United States lives in comparative self-sufficiency and isolation; Great Britain, in military security but economic dependence; and France, in greater economic independence but unusual military danger. Any conclusions reached with respect to them should have rather a broad validity.

In each of these countries the conduct of foreign relations is in the hands of the executive branch of government, and the executive is controlled in the exercise of this function by the people or by the people's representatives in the legislature. The executive in the United States consists of a president and a cabinet which is responsible to him alone. The president is elected for a fixed term by a practically direct choice of the people. He is constitutionally independent of the legislature, but the legislature has certain constitutional prerogatives connected with the conduct of foreign affairs. All treaties must be approved for ratification by a two-thirds vote of the Senate. The Senate must confirm appointments. The House must originate and the Congress pass all appropriations of public money. Treaties are part of the supreme law of the land, but when legislation is necessary to give them effect, it must be enacted by Congress. Subsequent congressional enactments supersede treaties.

In England and France the executive consists of a committee of the legislature representing the party or parties temporarily dominant therein. This executive serves only at the pleasure of the legislature. It retains power usually on the basis of its whole policy, domestic as well as foreign, but may be dismissed at any moment upon any particular point of policy. In both countries treaties of certain kinds must be approved by the legislature for ratification. Others, some of them very important, need not be. A treaty, however, has no validity as a law of the land unless it be given such by legislative action. Public moneys may be appropriated only by a vote of the legislature.

In the United States and France the legislature alone has power to declare war. In Great Britain this is a constitutional prerogative of the Crown, but in practice, we have seen, war cannot be begun, or having been begun, maintained except upon the basis of agreement between the executive and a substantial majority in the legislature.

In the United States the executive as well as the legislature is directly answerable to the people. In

Great Britain and France the executive is answerable to the legislature and the legislature to the people. The British executive may appeal directly to the people if it is not supported by the legislature on a particular issue. The French Chambers can be dissolved by agreement between the president and the senate, and this has been done once.

In all three governments there are some external matters as to which the executive is free from immediate constitutional interference by the legislature. The executives of Great Britain and France may conclude certain kinds of treaties on their own responsibility, notably treaties of alliance and other political engagements. The President of the United States, on the other hand, may pursue an independent foreign policy so far as neither treaties, appropriations, nor laws are requisite to its consummation. But the latitude of independent executive action is to a great extent theoretical. The ministries of Great Britain and France are answerable at all times to the legislature, and the President of the United States is the representative of the people no less than Congress. Dependence need not, moreover, be placed upon constitutional means alone. Experience has shown that for democracies the larger arrangements of external policy are illusive unless they accord with principles which the thought and instincts of the people approve. The Franco-Russian alliance was ratified by the public sentiment of France,[1] while an outburst of popular feeling in Italy made finally ineffective Italy's alliance with the Central Powers. An aroused public opinion becomes palpa-

[1] *Cf.* Barthélemy: *Démocratie et la politique étrangère,* pp. 229 and 230.

ble at once through the various and sundry channels we have noted, and, where the spirit of democracy lives, it controls, by constitutional means sometimes, often through the mere habit and desire of responsible officials to follow it.

I believe that in the countries which we ordinarily think of as democratic, effective means exist to control the executive conduct of foreign relations. The question is really not so much the existence of the means as their use. The essential fact is the indifference of the public to matters which are so often removed from their immediate interest and understanding. Only the later and more acute stages of foreign problems can be counted upon to command any general attention, and interest is then directed to the ends to be attained rather than the means.[2] Respecting many situations, especially in their initial stages, there is, as we have previously noticed, no public opinion at all, and the responsible officers of government must proceed in their discretion and in accordance with such guidance as they may find in tradition and precedent.

Representative democracy affords the practical expedient. The Supreme Court has said: "The idea is utopian that government can exist without leaving the exercise of discretion somewhere. Public security against the abuse of such discretion must rest upon responsibility, and stated appeals to the public approbation. Where all power is derived from the people, and public functionaries, at short intervals, deposit it at the feet of the people, to be resumed

[2] Note, for example, the tenor of the communications on the subject of disarmament addressed to the American delegation at the Washington Conference.

again only at their will, individual fears may be alarmed by the monsters of imagination, but individual liberty can be in little danger.'"[3] In the field of foreign affairs, having regard to the intricacy and vital importance of the matters dealt with and their removal from the immediate surroundings of domestic life, it is incumbent on the people to obtain the services of the most representative and resourceful among them, and it is the duty of those in whom this confidence is placed to keep the people fully and promptly informed in order that public opinion may crystallize for their guidance and control at the earliest moment and to the greatest extent that it will.

Inefficiency in the conduct of foreign relations has always been deemed to be the grave defect of democratic government. It is plain that, states being individuals in the family of nations, the individual or autocratic form of government has a certain tactical advantage in pursuing its international interests. It decides more readily what it wants and has the greatest freedom of action in seeking to obtain it. Democracy must feel its way, taking account not only of the international situation but of the inner workings of its own mind, which are sometimes cumbersome and slow. This very deliberateness imparts to democratic policy, however, a greater ultimate wisdom. The wisdom of autocracies, including in that term more or less autocratic oligarchies such as Imperial Germany, is the wisdom of the individual or the few and may be only self-delusion. Democracy,

[3] Justice Johnson in *Anderson v. Dunn,* 6 *Wheaton* 226, cited in Anderson, C. P.: *Extent and limitations of the treaty-making power,* in *Am. Jour. Int. Law,* 1: 636.

on the other hand, suffers from the liability of the multitude to sudden heats and sentimental impulses and long intervening periods of indifference. Representative democracy is again the practical expedient. By reposing confidence for brief periods in chosen leaders, it gains in tactical mobility, retains the balanced wisdom of deliberate popular feeling, lessens the danger of unwise impulses, and bridges the periods of popular indifference.

It is necessary to bear in mind that democratic government, especially in the realm of foreign affairs, has hardly passed the era of initial experiment. In the United States, where it has been longest on trial, foreign relations have been simple and relatively unimportant.[4] In France, where the conditions of external existence have, on the other hand, been especially difficult, it has also succeeded, though somewhat at the cost of the democratic dogma. The charge that foreign policy is the weak point of a democracy finds little support, says Bryce, in a study of French history between 1871 and 1914. French foreign policy has been conducted, he writes, "through many difficult crises, sometimes unwisely, yet with fewer variations of aim than have been visible in the lines followed by the other great European states. The two Chambers, in this respect reflecting and obeying the mind and purpose of the nation, have almost always strengthened and supported the Executive. When one considers the defects incident to the rule of popular assemblies, the

[4] For a good estimate of the success of the democratic experiment in the field of foreign relations, as exemplified by the history of the United States, see Fish, C. R.: *American diplomacy,* chap. xxxvi.

restraint which the Chambers imposed upon themselves must elicit the respect of impartial observers. . . . Greater errors were committed and more weakness shown under the Orleans Monarchy and certainly under the Second Empire.''[5]

The conduct of foreign relations in England, no less successful than in the past, has been marked during recent times, on the one hand, by survivals of the aristocratic tradition and, on the other, by radical progress in the democratic experiment, especially under Mr. Lloyd George, who introduced a new era of publicity, evinced an unprecedented readiness to follow the momentary shiftings of public desire, and in general popularized diplomacy with some bad and some good results.[6] Possibilities for the future have been suggested by a noticeable movement away from representative government toward direct action by the people or sections of them. So far the trend of these manifestations has been against a resumption of hostilities, but there is no conclusive evidence in history of a uniformly pacific disposition of the popular mind.

The conduct of foreign relations under the rapidly developing conditions of modern democracy is a vital and fascinating problem. Those who have faith in the democratic principle must suffer discouragement at times, rather through eagerness and impatience on their own part. The popular sense of responsibility and restraint which is essential to peace in a democratic world will grow as world

[5] *Modern democracies,* 1: 319. See chap. lxi of this work for a general estimate of democracy in its relation to foreign policy.

[6] *Cf.* Kennedy: *Old diplomacy and new,* Pt. III, chap. i, and the special appendix to the 2d ed.

affairs come increasingly within the popular knowledge, and the wisdom of the popular judgment, when it is deliberately expressed, is a foundation upon which a lasting edifice may be built.

INDEX

Adams, Charles Francis, 33 n.
Adams, Henry, 177 n.
Adams, John, quoted, 127 n.
  Works, 127 n.
Adams, John Quincy, 65 n.
Administrative organization, 55-60
  Denmark, 57-58
  France, 57
  Great Britain, 56-57, 58
  United States, 73-82
Advance Sheets of Consular Reports, 75
Africa, French policy in, 149
Alliances, international, 101
Almanach de Gotha, 24, 25 n.
American Commonwealth, The, 66, 66 n., 143, 144 n., 162 n., 164 n.
American Consular Bulletin, 60 n., 77 n.
American Consular Service, The, 73 n.
American Diplomacy, 195 n.
American Federation of Labor, 183
American Foreign Policy, 8 n.
American Journal of International Law, 11 n., 15 n., 16 n., 26 n., 27 n., 30 n., 63 n., 73 n., 120 n., 142 n., 163 n., 164 n.
American Party System, The, 176 n., 177 n.
American Political Science Review, 29 n., 44 n., 48 n., 76 n., 113 n., 137 n., 160 n., 168 n., 178 n., 181 n., 187 n.
American Society of International Law, 88 n.
Anderson, C. P., 63 n., 194 n.
Annam protectorate, 149.

Arbitration, 28 n.
  Permanent Court of, 86-87
Atlantic Monthly, 146 n.

Bacon, Senator Augustus O., quoted, 161
Baker, Ray Stannard, 37 n., 96 n., 104 n., 107 n., 136
  quoted, 103, 171-172
Balance of power, 101-102
Balfour, Arthur J., 46, 106 n., 147 n.
  note of Aug. 1, 1922, 31-32
  quoted, 96-97
Barnes, Julius, 139 n.
Barthélemy, Joseph, 44 n., 50 n., 110 n., 117 n., 128 n., 131 n., 152 n., 180 n., 192 n.
  quoted, 49, 99, 99-100, 116, 149-150, 154
Baruch, Bernard M., 159 n.
Bayard, Thomas F., 115 n.
Berlin Congress of 1878, 38, 95
Berlin, Treaty of, 149
Bernard, Mountague, quoted, 127
Bismarck, Otto E. L. von, 127
Blennerhasset, Sir Rowland, quoted, 8
Board of Trade Journal, 112
Borah, William E., 106 n., 165 n.
Bosphorus fortifications, Russian desire for, 34
Bouillon, Franklin, 30, 124 n.
Boursault, J. F., 98
Briand, Aristide, 13, 125, 159 n.
British and Foreign State Papers, 113
British Foreign Policy and the Dominions, 48 n.
British Yearbook of International Law, 48 n.

Brooks, Sydney, quoted, 8
Brown, Philip Marshall, 15 n.,
  quoted, 188-189, 189
Brunet, René, quoted, 52
Brusewitz, quoted, 53-54
Bryan, William Jennings, 27 n.
Bryce, James, 45 n., 50, 55, 66,
  122, 129 n., 130, 142 n., 143-
  144, 153, 162 n., 164, 175 n.,
  178 n.
  quoted, 137, 138, 139, 186-187,
  195-196
Bulletin officiel, 117

Cambacérès, Jean J. R. de, 98
Campaign issues, foreign policies
  as, 176-180
Cannes Conference, 13, 159 n.
Carey, Edward, 141 n.
Caribbean, American forces in,
  72
Carol, King of Rumania, 94
Carr, Wilbur J., 73 n.
Carson, Sir Edward, quoted, 155
  n.
Cecil, Lord Robert, 128
  quoted, 156 n., 158
Century of American Diplomacy,
  127 n.
Chamber of Commerce, 183-184
Charles, Garfield, 112 n.
Chautauqua, 135
Chester, Colby M., 30 n.
Chicherin, G., 34
  quoted, 38
China, 71, 72, 102
Choate, Joseph H., 66, 175
Chow, S. R., 47 n., 50 n., 150 n.,
  154 n., 163 n., 166 n.
Churchill, Winston, 153
Clemenceau, Georges, 128
Command Papers, 54 n.
Commerce, Department of, 75-76
Commerce Reports, 75, 76 n., 112

Commercial Bureau of American
  Republics, 86
Commercial information, 56-58
*Common Sense and Foreign
  Policy*, 126 n.
Concert of Europe, 85
Conciliation, 10
*Conduct of American Foreign Re-
  lations, The*, 62 n., 63 n., 64
  n., 65 n., 72 n., 150 n., 154 n.,
  164 n., 168 n., 185 n.
Conference of American States,
  First International, 85
Conferences, international, 34-40,
  34 n., 40 n.
  military, 35
Congressional Record, 106 n.,
  128 n., 139 n., 162 n., 165 n.
*Constitution allemande du 11 du
  août, 1919, La*, 52 n.
Constitutional Convention of
  1787, 104-105
Constitutional Law, 167 n.
Constitutional provisions, American, 62-72, 165, 190-192
  European, 41-55, 62, 99, 151-
  152, 165, 166 n., 180, 181,
  190-192
Contemporary Review, 46 n.
*Control of American Foreign Re-
  lations, The*, 29 n., 63 n., 64,
  65 n., 67 n., 68 n., 151 n.,
  161 n.
Control of Diplomacy, 63 n.
Control of Foreign Affairs, The,
  46 n.
*Control of Foreign Relations,
  The*, 29 n., 113 n., 137 n.,
  160 n.
*Contrôle parlementaire de la po-
  litique étrangère*, 47 n., 50
  n., 150 n., 154 n., 163 n., 166
  n.
Cook, Sir Edward, 126 n.

INDEX

Coolidge, Archibald C., and Pribram, A. F., 101 n.
Corwin, Edward S., 63 n., 65 n., 71 n., 72 n., 161 n., 162 n., 165 n., 167 n.
Council of Ambassadors, 85
Council of Four, 36
Council of Ten, 36
Council, Supreme, 85
Cours de droit diplomatique, 60 n.
Current History, 13 n., 33 n., 54 n., 99 n., 160 n.,
Curzon, George Nathaniel, Lord, 24, 123-124
quoted, 124

Danish Foreign Service Reorganized, 60 n.
Dardanelles fortifications, Russian desire for, 34
Debts, interallied, 31-32
Defence, British Committee of Imperial, 35
Deforgues, F. L. M. C., quoted, 32
Delane of the Times, 126 n.
Democracy and Diplomacy, 106 n., 147 n., 158 n., 159 n.
Démocratie et la politique étrangère, 44 n., 49 n., 50 n., 99 n., 110 n., 116 n., 117 n., 128 n., 131 n., 150 n., 152 n., 154 n., 180 n., 192 n.
Democratic Control of Foreign Policy, 146 n.
Dennis, A. L. P., 48 n.
Department of State, The, 73 n.
Department of State MSS. Despatches and Instructions, Great Britain, 33 n.
Department of State, United States, Foreign Service Announcement, 21 n.
de Thionville, Merlin, quoted, 98

Development of American Nationality, The, 178 n.
Dickinson, E. D., 8 n.
Dickinson, G. Lowes, quoted, 146
Digest of International Law, 12 n., 18 n., 40 n., 109 n., 115 n., 127 n.
Diplomacy and the Study of International Relations, 108 n.
Diplomacy of the Quarterdeck, 30 n.
Diplomacy Old and New, 117 n.
Diplomatic and Consular Services. See Foreign Service.
Diplomatic Correspondence, 33 n.
Diplomatic correspondence, publication of, 113-115
Diplomatic Correspondence of the American Revolution, 63 n.
Diplomatic Negotiations of American Naval Officers, 30 n.
Diplomatic Practice, 29 n., 34 n., 40 n.
Disraeli, Benjamin, 178, 186
Dominions, British, in foreign affairs, 47-48, 48 n.

Education, Bureau of, circular, 140 n.
Edward VII, 44 n.
Encyclopædia Britannica, 111
English Review, 8 n.
Equality of States in International Law, 8 n.
Essays on Some Disputed Questions in Modern International Law, 8 n.
Europe et la revolution française, 17 n., 32 n., 99 n.
Evening Standard, 187
Executive and Legislature, 117-120, 143-145, 165
political breaches of unity between, 13, 144-145

INDEX

See also Constitutional Provisions; Sovereign, personal influence of; Parliamentary control.
Experiments in International Administration, 84 n.
Extent and Limitations of the Treaty-Making Power, 63 n., 194 n.

Fashoda incident, 107-108
Federalist, 64 n.
Federation and Empire, 147 n.
Fiscal control, 152, 163, 164-167, 191
Fish, C. R., 178 n., 195 n.
Fishing rights on coasts of Canada and Newfoundland, 71
Fiume, Wilson appeal to abandon, 32
Foedera, 111
Force, 8-9
Foreign Affairs, 15 n., 54 n., 151 n.
Foreign Affairs Neglected Study, 139 n.
Foreign citizens, rights of, 4
Foreign Office Autocracy, 46 n.
Foreign Office List, British, 57
Foreign Policy, 8 n.
Foreign Policy Control in Norway, 54 n.
Foreign Relations, 113
Foreign Service, 20-21, 22-28, 58, 59, 60, 60 n., 89
  American, 21-22, 21 n., 27, 27 n., 73-82, 89, map inside back cover
  diplomatic personnel, 24-27, 59, 60
  duties of diplomats, 27-28 and notes
  extraordinary instrumentalities, 29-30
  map inside front cover

Foreign Service Changes World Wide, 60 n.
Fortnightly Review, 8 n., 46 n.
Forum, 106 n.
Foster, John W., 115 n., 127 n.
Four Power Treaty, 67-68
Free Thought and Official Propaganda, 127 n.
French Foreign Policy, 50 n.
French Revolution, 17, 97-99

Genet, Edmond C. E., 32
Genoa Conference, 13, 38, 159 n., 172
George V, 44 n.
George, David Lloyd, 13, 36, 44, 47, 61, 116, 125, 126 n., 153, 159, 159 n., 172, 173, 183, 196
Giolitti, Giovanni, 151
Giolitti's Bill to Abolish Secret Diplomacy, 151 n.
Given, John L., 133 n., 134 n.
Gladstone, William E., 45 n.
  quoted, 178
Government of England, The, 43 n., 44 n., 153 n.
Great Lakes, limitation of naval forces on, 71
Greeley, Horace, 170
Grew, Joseph C., 60 n.
Grey, Sir Edward, 12, 97, 153
  quoted, 44, 147 n., 158, 166, 168 n.
Grigg, Sir Edward, 130-131

Hague Conference of 1899, 86
Hague Conference of 1907, 5, 87
Hale, William Bayard, 30
Hall, A. B., 184 n.
Hamilton, Alexander, 120
Hankey, Sir Maurice, 35, 36
Hansard, 3d Series, 45 n.
Harding, Warren G., 6-70, 88, 116, 185

INDEX

Harper's Magazine, 27 n., 133 n.
Hay, John, 67, 161
  Life and Letters of, 66 n., 67 n., 161 n., 175 n.
  quoted, 18, 66, 160-161, 175
Hay-Pauncefote Treaty, 66, 160
Hearings, Committee, 120-121
Hearst papers, 173
Heatley, David P., 108 n.
Hendrick, Burton J., 13 n., 115 n.
Herriot, Mayor of Lyons, 30
Hertslet, Sir E., 117
Hill, David Jayne, 27 n.
History and Nature of International Relations, 28 n.
History of the United States during the First Administration of Madison, 177 n.
Holy Roman Empire, 3, 83
House, Colonel Edward M., 30
House Reports, 79 n.
House of Representatives, bills, 78 n., 79 n.
Hughes, Charles Evans, 15 n., 24, 25, 26 n., 27 n., 38, 39, 88 n., 89, 142 n., 159 n., 162
  quoted, 10-11, 27 n., 39, 69-70, 79-82, 118-120, 123, 164
Hunt, Gaillard, 73 n.
Husting, Senator Paul O., 184
Hyde, Charles C., 5 n., 12 n., 27-28 n., 88 n.

Information, public, 135-136, 138-141, 155-157
  See also Interest, public; Press; Propaganda; Publications; Public Utterances.
Institutes of the Law of Nations, The, 8
Interest, legislative, 145-146, 147, 149
  public, 129-136, 148-149, 193
International administrative bodies, 83-85

International Conciliation, 141 n.
International judicial organizations, 86-88
  See also World Court.
International Justice, Permanent Court of, 87-88, 88 n.
International Law (Hyde), 5 n., 12 n., 27-28 n., 88 n.
International Law (Oppenheim), 3 n., 5 n., 8 n., 12 n.
International political organizations, 85-86
International Prize Court, 87
International Realities, 189 n.
International Relations, 137 n., 139 n., 142 n., 153 n.
International Society, 15 n.
International Status of the British Self-Governing Dominions, The, 48 n.
Intervention in International Law, 5 n.
Introduction to the Study of International Organization, An, 85 n., 88 n.
Izvestia (Moscow), 9 n.

Japanese immigration, 71
Jefferson, Thomas, 189
Johnson, Hiram, 38 n.
Johnson, Justice William, quoted, 193-194
Johnston, Sir Harry, 126 n.
Journalism and International Affairs, 141 n.
Journalism and International Politics, 133 n.

Kemal, Mustapha, 30, 124 n.
Kennedy, Aubrey L., 96 n., 97 n., 107-108, 155 n., 159 n., 179 n., 183 n., 196 n.
  quoted, 108, 125-126

Labour Council of Action, 183
Lambert, Rt. Hon. George, 159 n.

Lansing, Robert, 14, 33
  quoted, 11-12, 32
Lausanne Conference, 34, 123-124, 124
Law, Bonar, 170, 187
  quoted, 168 n.
Lawrence, T. J., quoted 8 n.
League of Nations, 14, 85, 86, 102, 128, 176, 177, 181, 182, 183
League of Women Voters, 140
Lectures on Diplomacy, 127 n.
Legislature and Executive. *See* Executive and Legislature.
Legislatures and Foreign Relations, 168 n., 178 n., 187 n.
Lewis, M. M., 48 n.
Liberum veto, the, 5-6
Lichnowsky, Karl M., quoted, 97
Limitation of Armament. *See* Washington Conference.
Limitation of naval forces on the Great Lakes, 71
Lincoln, Abraham, 33 n.
  Complete Works, 33 n.
Lind, John, 30
Lippmann, Walter, 129 n., 133 n., 134 n., 135 n., 188
  quoted, 135-136, 137 n., 153
Literary Digest, 186
Living Age, 182 n., 186
Lodge, Henry C., 69, 74
London, Declaration of, 163
London, Meyer, quoted, 139
London Gazette, 112
London *Times*, 126, 173, 174
L'Opinion, 186
Lorimer, James, quoted, 8
Low, Sidney, 46 n.
Lowell, Abbott Lawrence, 44 n., 129 n., 141, 153 n., 166, 183 n.
  quoted, 43, 104, 105-106, 179-180
Lucking, Alfred, 183 n.

McBain, H. L., and Rogers, L., 44 n., 47 n., 54 n., 99 n., 172 n.
MacClintock, Samuel, 76 n.
McClure's Magazine, 159 n., 162 n.
Macdonald, Ramsay, quoted, 168 n.
McKellar, Senator Kenneth D., 106 n.
McKinley, William, 69
MacNeill, Swift, quoted, 166, 167
Madison, James, 62 n., 67
Making a Newspaper, 133 n., 134 n.
Making of the Reparations and Economic Sections of the Treaty, The, 159 n.
Malloy, William M., 15 n., 112
Margaine, A., 176 n.
Mathews, John M., 63 n., 64 n., 65 n., 72 n., 150-151, 154 n., 164 n., 167-168, 185 n.
  quoted, 62 n.
Mediation, 4, 28, 28 n.
Merriam, Charles E., 176 n., 177 n.
Messages, Presidential, 120
Mexican policy, 161
Michon, Louis, 42 n., 150 n.
Ministerial responsibility, 20, 43-45, 49, 61, 65-66, 152, 155 n., 157, 190, 191-192, 193
Modern Democracies, 50 n., 66, 66 n., 129 n., 130 n., 138 n., 142 n., 153 n., 175 n., 178 n., 187 n., 196 n.
Moore, John Bassett, 12 n., 18, 28 n., 40 n., 71 n., 109 n., 115 n., 127 n.
Morel, Edmund D., 151 n.
Morrell, Philip, 46 n.
Mudania Conference, 124 n.
Muir, Ramsay, 15 n.

INDEX

Myers, Denys P., 29 n., 114-115
   quoted, 113, 136-137, 160, 168 n.
My Mission to London, 97 n.

Napoleon III, 94
Nation, The, 63 n., 106 n.
National Vote on the League, A, 183 n.
Nationalism, 14-16, 141
Nationalism and Internationalism, 15 n.
Need for a Popular Understanding of International Law, The, 16 n.
Negotiation, 28, 28 n.
New Constitutions of Europe, The, 44 n., 47 n., 54 n., 99 n., 172 n.
New York *Times*, 5 n., 32 n., 38 n., 51 n., 124 n., 126 n., 139 n., 182 n., 184 n., 185 n., 186 n., 187 n.
   See also Current History.
New York *Tribune*, 125 n.
North American Review, 67
Northcliffe, Lord, 173
Nouvelle Revue, 176 n.

Old Diplomacy and New, 96 n., 97 n., 107, 126 n., 155 n., 159 n., 179 n., 183 n., 196 n.
Oppenheim, L. F. L., 3 n., 5 n., 6, 7, 8 n., 12 n.
   quoted, 10
Oregon Treaty, 69
Orlando, V. E., quoted, 32-33
Our World, 183 n.

Page, Walter Hines, 12
   Life and Letters, 13 n., 115 n.
Palmerston, Lord, 117
Pan-American Union, 85-86, 86 n.
   Report of the Director General, 86 n.

Papacy, 3
Paris Peace Conference, 36-37, 103-104, 107, 128
Parliament and Foreign Policy, 166 n.
Parliamentary control of foreign affairs, 43-47 n., 144, 151-152, 155-168
   British Dominions, 47-48
   France, 48-51, 163, 191
   Germany, 51-52
   Great Britain, 43-48, 46 n., 147 n., 156-157, 157-159, 191
   Prevailing Continental system, 54-55
   Sweden, 52-54, 54 n.
   United States, 65-73, 150-151, 160-168, 190, 191
   See also Constitutional provisions; Treaty-making power.
Parliamentary Control of Foreign Affairs in Sweden, 54 n.
Parliamentary Debates, Commons, 46 n., 97 n., 106 n., 116 n., 117 n., 127 n., 137 n., 146 n., 147 n., 156 n., 158 n., 159 n., 166 n., 172 n.
   Lords, 38 n., 172 n.
Parliamentary Government in England, 157 n., 166 n., 167 n.
Parliamentary Papers, 114
Parliamentary questions, 116-117, 117 n.
Paullin, Charles O., 30 n.
Pauncefote, Sir Julian, 66, 160
Peace Negotiations, The, 14 n., 33 n.
Peace note of 1916, German, 35
Pedersen, 54 n.
Pepper, Senator George W., 38 n.
Perils of Secret Treaty-Making, The, 106 n.
Perry, Stuart H., quoted, 67-68
Phillips, Williams, 77 n.

Plebiscite, 180-183
Poincaré, Raymond, 13, 24, 51 n., 115, 121, 170
Political parties and foreign affairs, 12-13, 68, 69, 74, 144-145, 147 n., 153-155, 174-176, 179-180
See also Campaign issues.
Political Parties and Foreign Policy in France, 175 n.
Political Science Quarterly, 71 n.
Politique extérieure de la France et la parti radical, La, 176 n.
Polk, James K., 69, 178
Pomeroy, Prof. J. N., 167 n.
Ponsonby, Arthur A. W. H., 106 n., 116 n., 117 n., 146, 147 n., 158 n., 159
quoted, 137
Popular Government, 184 n.
Potter, Pitman B., 85 n., 88 n.
Powers, Great, 6
Ambassadors of, in 1922, 25 n.
Practice of Diplomacy, The, 115 n.
Pradier-Fodéré, P. L. E., quoted, 40, 60
President's Control of Foreign Relations, The, 63 n., 65 n., 71 n., 72 n., 161 n., 162 n., 165 n., 167 n.
Press bureaus, official, 122, 127 n.
Press conferences and interviews, 122-126
Press in international relations, 30-34, 107
Press opinion, influence of, 170-174
Press, spread of information through, 121-128, 132-137, 174
Pribram, A. F., and Coolidge, A. C., 101 n.
Primacy of the Great Powers, 8 n.
Propaganda, 127-128

Publications, official, 110-115
Publicity, advantages and disadvantages of, 30-34, 93-96, 103-109, 155 n.
Public Opinion, 129 n., 133 n., 134 n., 135 n., 136 n.
Public opinion, group and individual expression of, 183-189
sounding of, 30-34
weight of, 192-193
See also Referendum.
Public Opinion and Popular Government, 129 n., 141 n., 180 n.
Public Opinion in War and Peace, 104, 106 n., 129 n., 166 n., 183 n.
Public utterances, official, 115-121

Recognition of foreign governments, 70-71
Recouly, Raymond, quoted, 133
Referendum, 180-183
Reparations, Lloyd George and "Khaki" parliament on, 159
Requisite for the Success of Popular Diplomacy, A, 15 n.
"Reservations" of legislature, 150
Resolutions, advisory, of State legislatures, 184-185
Riddell, Lord George A., 124, 125
Rise of Democracy, The, 179 n.
Rogers, L., and McBain, H. L., 44 n., 47 n., 54 n., 99 n., 172 n.
Rogers bill, 78-82
Rome Conference, Christmas, 1916, 35
Roosevelt, Theodore, 9, 74
Theodore Roosevelt: An Autobiography, 9 n.

INDEX

Root, Elihu, 74
  Address of Jan. 17, 1923, 5 n., 15 n.
  quoted, 4-5, 15 n., 16, 87
Rose, J. Holland, 179 n.
Rosebery, Lord, quoted, 154-155
Round Table, The, 35
Ruhr, 4, 170
Rush-Bagot agreement, 71
Russell, Bertrand, quoted, 127
Russell, Earl John, 33 n.
Russell, Lord Odo, quoted, 38
Russian policy, 161
Russian Soviet, 4, 17, 34, 183
Rymer's *Foedera*, 111

Salisbury, Lord, 95, 107-108, 179
  quoted, 108
Satow, Sir Ernest M., 29, 34, 34 n.
Sayre, Francis B., 84 n.
Secret Diplomacy, 106 n.
Secret Treaties of Austria Hungary, The, 101 n.
Self-interest, 8-12
Senate documents, 112 n., 121 n.
Sensationalism, 137-138
Sentiment in public opinion, 141
Seward, William H., quoted, 33 n.
Shall We Standardize Our Diplomatic Service? 27 n.
Some Aspects of the Work of the Department of State, 27 n.
Some Observations on the Conduct of Our Foreign Relations, 11 n., 15 n., 26 n., 142 n.
Sorel, Albert, 17 n., 32 n., 97, 99 n.
Sovereign or executive, personal influence of, 43, 44 n., 50, 94, 144, 162, 188, 192
  American executive, 63-65, 69-72, 118, 160, 192

Sovereign states, equality of, 6-8, 8 n.
  independence of, 3-5, 5 n.
Spain, 138
  United States treaty with, 69
Spalding, T. A., 147 n.
Specific Agencies for the Proper Conduct of International Relations, 28 n.
Stakes of Diplomacy, The, 137 n., 153 n., 188 n.
Statutes at Large, 73 n., 74 n., 76 n., 165 n.
Steel-Maitland, Sir Arthur, 56
Stowell, E. C., 5 n.
Stuart, Graham H., quoted, 50

Taft, William Howard, quoted, 119
Tardieu, André, 170
Temps, Le (Paris), 126, 170, 173
Thayer, William Roscoe, 66 n., 67, 161 n., 175 n.
Thomas, T. H., 175 n.
Tocqueville, A. C. H. M. C. de, 189
Todd, Alpheus, 166 n., 167 n.
  quoted, 156-157
Torretta, P. Tomasi della, 24, 26
Trade information, 56-58
Traités internationaux devant les chambres, Les, 42 n., 150 n.
Transvaal Government, 138
Treaties, 29, 67, 148-151, 180, 181
  publication of, 110-112
  secret, 94, 95, 96-99, 102, 181
Treaties, 111
Treaties, Conventions, etc., 112
Treaties and Executive Agreements, 71 n.
Treatment of International Questions by Parliaments in European Countries, the United States and Japan, 54 n.

Treaty-making power, 41, 41 n.
　British Dominions, 47-48
　France, 48-51, 150, 191, 192
　Great Britain, 43-48, 191, 192
　Latvia, 41 n.
　Spain, 41 n.
　Swiss referendum, 55
　United States, 62-70, 148-149, 150-151, 191
　See also Constitutional provisions; Parliamentary control.
Turner, E. R., 63 n.
Tyler, John, 178

Uchida, Yasuya, 24
Underwood, Oscar W., 69
Unified Foreign Service, A, 76 n.
Unions, international administrative, 84-85

Versailles, Treaty of, 36, 67-68, 69, 84 n., 120, 149, 186
Victoria, 44 n.
Vienna, Congress of, 1815, 6

Walsh, Edmund A., 28 n.
War-making power, 163, 165-168, 180, 191
Washington, George, 69, 189
Washington Conference, 5, 31, 37, 69, 102, 165, 185
Washington *Post*, 34 n., 121 n., 170 n.
Webster-Ashburton Treaty, 16
Wharton, Francis, 63 n.
White, Henry, 160
Williams, Consul H. O., 60 n.
Wilson, Woodrow, 14, 32, 33, 36, 96, 188
　quoted, 101-102, 103-104
Woodrow Wilson and the World Settlement, 37 n., 96 n., 104 n., 107 n., 136 n., 172 n.
Working for Mexico, 185 n.
World Court, 70, 162, 185
World's Work, 175 n.
Wright, Quincy, 29 n., 63 n., 64-65, 67 n., 68 n., 151 n., 161 n.

Young, George, 117 n.